Twelve Locals and a South African

© Copyright Widnes Rl

Photos as credited. All photographs copyright
intentionally breached any copyright. If any ph
please contact the publishers.

This book is copyright under the Berne Convention. All rights are reserved. It is sold subject to the condition that it shall not, by way of trade or otherwise, be lent resold, hired out or otherwise circulated without the publisher's prior consent in any form of binding or cover other than that in which it is published and without a similar condition being imposed on the subsequent purchaser.

A CIP catalogue record for this book is available from the British Library.

First published in Great Britain by Widnes RLFC Limited in July 2005.

ISBN: PB: 0-9550762-0-x
             HB: 0-9550762-1-8

Designed by: Tobin Design Ltd
                97 Highfield Road
                Widnes
                Cheshire WA8 7DH

Manufactured in the EU by L.P.P.S. Ltd, Wellingborough, Northants NN8 3PJ.

This book is dedicated to the game of Rugby League and all those involved in it.

Acknowledgements

The idea of this book came from a conversation I had with Ann Steel, a Widnes fan without whom the Vikings in the Community project would never have happened.

From then it was thanks to the efforts of Steph Davies (Halton BC), Andy Kelly (Heritage Lottery Fund) and Terry Parle (Halton Rugby League Service Area) that the funding was sourced.

At Sts Peter Paul, the English teachers, Jean Byrne and Jane Hines gave up a lot of their own time as, of course, did their pupils.

Mixed ability groups were determined by the teachers to write the chapters and it is hoped that this book reflects the hard work put in by the children. Some of the work has been amended to make the book 'flow' but I hope it does not take away from the aim of the project over what has been a very enjoyable 18 months.

This book could not have been produced without the contributions from the interviewees and I would like to thank them for giving their time without question.

Thanks must go to Widnes' Managing Director, Tom Fleet, for supplying a lot of the memorabilia as well as the brief history of the Club and Rod Steele who arranged the interview with Peter Spencer in Burnley.

Thanks must also go to Steve Fox for his contributions, Michele Carter for her research which has been a great help, Stuart Bogg at The Widnes Weekly News and Frank Tobin Jnr and John Birchall at Tobin Design Ltd who have turned pages and pages of text into this masterpiece you are about to read!

Pat Cluskey July 2005

The Writers

Matthew Atherton, Paul Boardman, James Davidson, Laura Devery, Calum Dunlop, Laura Griffiths, Rachel Grogan, Amanda Hayes, Kenny Hudson, Kayleigh Jerram, Alex Jones, Mark Leedam, Jak Lyons, Samantha McCormick, Lisa McKeown, Sarah Morley, Alan Murphy, Gary Nicholls, Michelle O'Brien, James O'Neill, Carla Owens, Lynsey Pich, David Prescott, Megan Rolt, Jenny Shard, Aimee Stewart, Kirsty Welding, Callum Whitby, Matthew Whittle and Anthony Woodward.

The Contributors

Chris Anderson, Brian Clarke, Pat Cluskey, Jonathan Davies, Ray Dutton, Tom Fleet, Mike Flynn, John Foran, Steve Fox, Ray French, Robert Gate, Paul Hansbury, Paul Hulme, Doug Laughton, Joe Lydon, Jim Mills, Frank Myler, Steve O'Neill, Jessie Rawlinson, Peter Spencer and Frank Tobin Snr.

Contents

Foreword 2
1930 v St Helens 3
1934 v Hunslet 13
1937 v Keighley 19
1950 v Warrington 27
1964 v Hull KR 35
1975 v Warrington 45
1976 v St Helens 55
1977 v Leeds 63
1979 v Wakefield 69
1981 v Hull KR 77
1982 v Hull 85
1984 v Wigan 95
1993 v Wigan 103
Brief History of Widnes RLFC 113

Foreword

Growing up in Widnes in the 70s / 80s was great if you were a fan of the Chemics. The town's rugby league team was known as the 'Cup Kings' during this era as they amassed trophy after trophy.

The major prize was the Rugby League Challenge Cup and I remember the excitement of my first visit to Wembley Stadium as a 10 year old, with my mum, to witness the defeat of Warrington in 1975.

It seemed to me as if the whole town was there to witness the victory and despite our train breaking down on the way home the spirit and camaraderie of both sets of fans was magnificent.

I made many more journeys to watch Widnes at Wembley over the years, initially with my dad, but as I got older with friends, and in 1993 as part of the official party, and each occasion provided me with great memories.

Having read the chapters written by the pupils of Sts Peter Paul RC High School not only are these memories rekindled but a picture of the scenes from 1930 onwards has been clearly painted in my mind and having recently witnessed Liverpool FC's homecoming with the Champions League trophy I can imagine similar scenes in Runcorn and Widnes 75 years ago.

Pat Cluskey

**1930 RUGBY LEAGUE CHALLENGE CUP FINAL
ST HELENS V WIDNES**
Saturday 3 May 1930, Wembley Stadium, London

1930 The Road to Wembley

The start of the season had not looked too rosy for the young Widnes team. They then broke a long-standing club 'rule' and decided to take a player from outside the district. They had always strictly adhered to a policy of local talent, but when Wigan came along with the generous offer of George Van Rooyen *(right)*, the great South African second row forward, as a gift on a free transfer, The Chemics gladly accepted.

Below: Jimmy Hoey (inset) and kicking for goal in the 1930 Wembley Final

Widnes had rarely been in a position up to that stage to pay big wages to their players, and stood by their determination not to squander money on transfer fees but to foster and rely upon local talent.

But the arrival of Van Rooyen proved a success of exciting proportions. His influence on the young side was immense from the start, and the part played by the big fellow (he was 6ft 2ins tall and weighed 16 stones) in Widnes' great run to Wembley was significant. All this at the age of 37.

Van Rooyen surprised every team in the league by his wonderful play, he was one of the cleanest players in the code and he quickly felt a part of the Widnes squad as his humorous personality shone. Even on the field he worked like a Trojan, always where the fight was thickest.

Having noted the success of the first ever Rugby League Challenge Cup Final to be held at Wembley Stadium the previous season, there was an added incentive for clubs as they entered the first round draw in 1930.

Previously the Finals had been staged in the North. Some of the grounds included Leeds, Oldham and Manchester but in 1929, the Rugby League had taken the momentous decision to move the game's most prestigious event to the finest possible setting. Wigan and Dewsbury had savoured the honour of being the first Finalists to tread the Wembley turf.

Widnes had opened the tournament in that memorable year with a comfortable 20-0 home win against Bradford Northern but the next round brought a tough battle to overcome Swinton. The sides drew 7-7 at Station Road. Widnes' next obstacle was to defeat Swinton in the replay which they did squeezing home 6-5 and the thoughts of their supporters were already turning towards the exciting prospect of an appearance in the Final and the trip to the new venue, Wembley Stadium.

Things were looking positive for the Chemics at this stage of the competition. The Quarter Final saw a home tie with Hull and a 19-5 victory saw the Chemics reach the last four.

Above: The history making 1930 Widnes team and officials

The idea of reaching the Wembley Final was an exciting prospect but first, a difficult Semi Final hurdle had to be overcome against Barrow. The match was set for Warrington and 25,500 people turned out for the occasion, bringing in handsome receipts for that time of £1,630. Widnes did not disappoint their loyal following and when the whistle sounded at the end of the eighty minutes, the cheers of the Widnes fans were said to be heard way back in their home town as the Chemics defeated Barrow 10-3.

The dream of playing at Wembley became a reality!

But who would Widnes face? Wigan were making another mighty effort to repeat their historic 1929 success but in the Semi-Final they were locked in a gruelling battle against St Helens, with the score ending 5-5 in front of a crowd of 37,000 at Swinton.

The replay was staged at Leigh and St Helens snatched the Wembley date from Wigan's hands to face their neighbours Widnes by triumphing 22-10 including two tries from Alf Ellaby, one of the greatest wingmen the game of Rugby League has ever known.

The Game

Peter Spencer was 7 years old at the time and can well remember the build up to the big day out. "Saints had a player called Ellaby who could 'catch pigeons' and the papers were full of what the Saints team were going to do to Widnes. They thought we were just going to make up the numbers.

"In those days there were no electric lights just gas lamps and all through the town effigies of Ellaby were hung from these lamps. It made the front pages of the local papers and also the Daily Despatch!

"What Saints hadn't accounted for was our secret weapon, George Van Rooyen. He'd come over from South Africa and played at Wigan but they thought he was past his sell by date so farmed him off to Widnes.

"I remember he was a tanker driver at ICI and when the fans collected to buy the ground for Widnes he got dressed up as a Zulu, wearing ostrich feathers and carrying spears. He must have made a couple of hundred pound dressed like that.

"Nobody had a TV in those days, in fact not everybody had radios but I did manage to hear the game. Everyone had a copy of the 'Radio Times' and in it there was a diagram of the pitch, divided into sections. The commentator on the radio would then tell the listeners where play was by saying which square it was in."

Below: Paddy Douglas (holding the Cup) and the victorious Widnes team parade the Challenge Cup

So as the 12 locals plus a South African took to the field at Wembley they were faced by a Saints team comprising nine Lancastrians, three New Zealanders and a Welshman and it was no surprise when after three minutes a kick from Alf Ellaby was touched down by Lou Houghton for the opening try.

However from the restart George Van Rooyen took the game by the scruff of the neck. "Van Rooyen knocked heck out of them" said Mr Spencer.

Within four minutes Widnes had taken the lead with a penalty try as Albert Ratcliffe was obstructed chasing his own kick. Jimmy Hoey, who a few years later became famous as the first player to play and score in every match of a season, added the goal.

As the first half drew to a close Widnes increased their lead through winger Jack Dennett and although Widnes couldn't land the conversion Ratcliffe did add a penalty to give the underdogs a 10-3 interval lead, a lead they were to hold onto for the 40 minutes of the second half as they out-played their more illustrious neighbours.

1930 RUGBY LEAGUE CHALLENGE CUP FINAL
Saturday 3 May 1930, Wembley Stadium, London

ST HELENS	T	G	P	WIDNES	T	G	P
	1	0	3		2	2	10
C. E. Crooks				R. Fraser			
A. Ellaby				J. Dennett	1		
W. Mercer				A. Ratcliffe	1	1	
G. Lewis				P. Topping			
R. A. Hardgrave				H. Owen			
L. Fairclough				P. Douglas Capt			
W. Groves				J. Laughton			
L. Hutt				F. Kelsall			
W. Clarey				G. Stevens			
L. Houghton	1			N. Silcock			
E. T. Hall				G. Van Rooyen			
B. Halfpenny				H. Millington			
R. Harrison				J. Hoey		1	

Referee: F Peel (Bradford)
Half Time: 3-10; Attendance: 36,544

Above: The victorious Widnes team mark their homecoming in grand style

The Homecoming

The homecoming for the Widnes team was greater than that for any Royal visit to the town as all sections of the community wanted to honour those players who had brought honour to the town.

A crowd, estimated to be in the tens of thousands, welcomed the team at Runcorn Station on the Monday evening following the game. The Chairman of Runcorn Urban District Council, Mr J. M. Holt was on the station platform to give the players an official welcome to Runcorn saying the people of Runcorn were proud of them and just as pleased as Widnes.

Also on board the train were the St Helens team and as the train pulled off for Liverpool both sets of players cheered each other. The players made their way to the front of the station to take their seats in a coach with the officials boarding a second coach. The players and committeemen were surprised at the warmth of the reception from the Runcornians and delighted that the Runcorn Silver Band, assisted by members of the Pioneer Band, had joined the parade.

As the coaches passed through the throngs they reached the Transporter Bridge where another big crowd had assembled and Van Rooyen, standing up in the coach, gave a war cry! Earlier in the day the townsfolk of Widnes busied themselves in preparing the town for the players. Lime and chalkstone were used to decorate houses and gable ends whilst black and white paper streamers festooned every street.

Banners were hung across the streets with messages such as "The Chemics Beat The Classics", "Van, the magician", "The Miner's dream of Wembley" and "We want the cup and we've got it"

Below: Homeward bound... the victorious 1930 Widnes team at Euston Station, London

As they reached the Widnes side of the river it seemed impossible for the procession to make its way through West Bank to the town centre as the crowds were too dense.

Eventually mounted police with a large body of sergeants and constables managed to clear a way and led by St Aidan's Band the coaches moved slowly through the crowd. The players were in the first of these coaches with Paddy Douglas holding aloft the Cup, the officials were in the second and a third coach had been arranged for members of the Town Council.

It took half an hour to reach the centre of the town and as the Town Hall Square was so packed the coaches made a detour along Kingsway and Moor Lane to Lowerhouse Lane and the ground.

Speeches were made by Douglas and then Van Rooyen who, according to the Mayor had been 'naturalised' at a ceremony in London.

"I only want to tell you that there is no happier man in the world tonight than me. There has been no prouder man to play with a team like these boys and bring the Cup. Determination everytime," said the South African.

Above: Widnes captain Paddy Douglas received an official welcome in the Council Chamber

The parade continued from the football field through the town to the Town Hall where the players received an official welcome in the Council Chamber where Paddy Douglas was installed in the Mayoral Chair and addressed as "Your Worship".

**1934 RUGBY LEAGUE CHALLENGE CUP FINAL
HUNSLET V WIDNES**
Saturday 5 May 1934, Wembley Stadium, London

1934 The Road to Wembley

The 1934 Challenge Cup campaign started with a home game against Leeds which saw the Chemics win by 12-3 followed by a trip to Hull Kingston Rovers in the second round, a game the visitors won 10-0.

The Quarter Final saw the Chemics travel over the Pennines again, this time to Halifax where they won a close game 5-3 to earn a Semi-Final spot against Oldham at Station Road, Swinton.

The game at Swinton was another close run affair with the Chemics defeating their Lancastrian counterparts 7-4 in front of a crowd of over 17,500.

Widnes' opponents in the 1934 Final were Hunslet whose path to the Final had begun with an 8-6 victory at Leigh. In the second round they travelled to Castleford where they drew 4-4 before a comprehensive 23-0 win in the replay.

In their Quarter Final they edged out York 2-0 before beating Huddersfield 12-7 in the Semi-Final at Wakefield in front of a crowd of nearly 27,500.

The Game

The Widnes party, including the Mayor and Mayoress, were invited to the Houses of Parliament by Mr Alex Cameron, the former Labour member for Widnes on the afternoon of their arrival in London. The Mayor thanked Mr Cameron for his interest in the team and hoped it would have the same effect as it had in 1930

Having won the Challenge Cup four years previously Widnes went into the Final against Hunslet in good heart although the team showed eight changes from the one that defeated St Helens.

The game was barely five minutes old when from a scrum on the Hunslet goal-line second rower Hugh McDowell crashed over for the game's opening try. Widnes' lead was reduced to just one point with a penalty goal from Hunslet's prop forward Mark Tolson.

Above:
Widnes captain
Nat Silcock

Below:
Harry Millington

Below right:
Peter Topping

The Yorkshiremen took the lead towards the end of the first half thanks to an unconverted try from centre Morrell which saw him break his collar bone in the act of scoring and take no further part in the game.

Early in the second half Widnes drew level with a penalty goal from second row Ratcliffe but that was to be the end of the Widnes scoring as tries from Hunslet's forwards Beverley and Smith gave victory to the Yorkshire outfit by 11-5.

After the game there was a dinner held in the Holborn Restaurant where the tables were decorated in black and white and despite their defeat the dinner was a 'triumph of the sporting spirit of Widnes players and officials who, giving full credit to the winners, showed by speech and demeanour that they could be excellent losers'.

Lord Derby attended the dinner and passed on best wishes from the King who was unable to attend the Challenge Cup Final but asked Lord Derby to pass on his thoughts that he would have been delighted if Widnes had won the Challenge Cup as Widnes was a team of Widnes men.

Nat Silcock, the Widnes captain made a great speech whilst acknowledging the fact that he was the most disappointed Lancastrian in London that night, he was sure that the majority of the young Widnes team would return to Wembley in the near future although he had doubts about whether or not he would.

For an 11 year old Peter Spencer it was heart-breaking, "It was the biggest disgrace ever, especially as Hunslet played half the game with 12 men. The problem was the Widnes team thought they just had to turn up to win. People said they were out on the razz the night before, if they were they deserved to lose."

Above: Harry Owen

1934 RUGBY LEAGUE CHALLENGE CUP FINAL
Saturday 5 May 1934, Wembley Stadium, London

HUNSLET	T	G	P	WIDNES	T	G	P
	3	1	11		1	1	5
J. Walkington				W. Bradley			
G. Dennis				H. Owen			
C. Morrell	1			P. Topping			
E. Winter				P. Jacks			
G. Broughton				A. Gallimore			
G. Todd				T. Shannon			
W. S. Thornton				T. McCue			
M. Tolson		1		N. Silcock Capt			
L. White				J. Jones			
L. Smith	1			A. Higgins			
H. Crowther				H. McDowell	1		
F. Dawson				A. Ratcliffe		1	
H. Beverley	1			H. Millington			

Referee: A Holbrook (Warrington)
Half Time: 5-3; Attendance: 41,280

The Homecoming

Having returned victorious in 1930 nobody in the Widnes party knew what to expect as they had lost.

They needn't have worried. Large crowds had gathered at Runcorn railway station on the Monday evening and the crowds lined the route from Runcorn to Widnes Town Hall. The players had travelled by train from London Euston and boarded coaches at Runcorn for the journey via the Transporter Bridge to Widnes.

At the Town Hall the crowd was so big that both mounted and foot police had great difficulty in keeping the crowds back from the road to enable the coaches to reach the square in front of the Town Hall.

As the players disembarked from the coaches each received a large cheer from the crowd. With the players now outside the Town Hall a band began to play and its first song was 'Happy Days Are Here Again' which had been adopted as the Widnes song.

The players spent a long time enjoying the occasion and signing autographs for their fans.

FINAL TIE

OF THE RUGBY LEAGUE CHALLENGE CUP COMPETITION

AT THE

EMPIRE STADIUM WEMBLEY

SATURDAY, MAY 8, 1937

CORONATION YEAR OF THEIR MAJESTIES
KING GEORGE VI AND QUEEN ELIZABETH

KEIGHLEY
v.
WIDNES

Kick-off 3 p.m.

OFFICIAL PROGRAMME SIXPENCE

1937 The Road to Wembley

With one Challenge Cup victory and one loss the 1937 campaign began with an easy tie against Oldham amateurs Higginshaw which the Chemic won 39-2 at Naughton Park.

This led to a home tie against Dewsbury in the second round. Widnes led 8-0 at half-time but the referee abandoned the game due to wintery weather. Fortunately for Widnes when the game was replayed they defeated Dewsbury 12-7.

In the Quarter Finals Widnes had yet another home tie, this time against Swinton a game they won 7-2 to earn a Semi-Final spot against Wigan.

The Semi-Final took place at Wilderspool Stadium, Warrington and in front of a crowd of over 29,000 Widnes won 13-9 to claim a place in their third Final in seven years.

This time Widnes' opponents were Keighley who began their route to the Final with a 5-2 victory at Hunslet before defeating Broughton Rangers at home by 11-5 in the second round.

WIDNES RLFC 1937

In the Quarter Final they travelled to Liverpool Stanley winning 7-2 before taking on Wakefield in the semis. This game was played at Headingley Stadium in front of just under 40,000 fans and at the end of 80 minutes the score was 0-0.

A replay followed at Fartown, Huddersfield and 14,000 people witnessed a Keighley victory by 5-3

The Game

Peter Spencer, now 14, went to his first Wembley Final this year. "I'd just left school and my dad, who was the steward of the Birmingham Corrugated Iron Club organized a fathers and sons trip. I travelled in the luggage rack and I can remember the fare being 5 shillings.

"We got onto the train at the LMS station in South Widnes and we were shunted to Ditton Junction where we hooked up with the London train. We should have gone straight to Wembley but for some reason the train went to Euston and we had to get buses to Wembley from there.

"Before the game there had been talk of Widnes playing in white shirts and black shorts with a gold crown on the shirts in honour of the King's Coronation, with Keighley wearing red, white and blue hoops but for some reason this didn't happen."

There was a nervous start to the 1937 Final with both sides struggling to get a grip on the game. However, eight minutes into the game Widnes won a scrum on the Keighley '25' and scrum half Tommy McCue stepped through several defenders before passing to Tommy Shannon who despite not taking the ball cleanly was able to regather it and touchdown for a try converted by Peter Topping.

Below: 'The Two Tommies' - Tommy Shannon (left) and Tommy McCue pose in their Lancashire kit outside the Naughton Park Pavilion

County and International scrum-half Tommy McCue, with some of the trophies he won during seventeen years as a playing member of the Widnes Rugby Football Club.

Widnes Weekly News photo.

Above: The legendary Tommy McCue with some of the trophies he won during his playing career at Widnes

McCue was the instigator of the second try for the Chemics as he intercepted a pass in the Keighley half and side stepped two defenders to touch down for a fantastic solo try to give Widnes an 8-0 interval lead.

Two minutes into the second half Keighley pulled two points back with a penalty goal after Widnes had been caught offside. This inspired the Keighley side but despite a tremendous amount of pressure the black and white defence held firm.

Widnes extended the lead when a Keighley attack failed as the ball went to ground and it was picked up by centre Ken Barber who raced away to touchdown, Topping landing the conversion to give Widnes a 13-2 lead.

The game was made safe five minutes later when a break from Harry Millington created the opportunity for Nat Silcock, who three years earlier had doubted he'd ever play at Wembley again, to touch down.

Although Topping was unsuccessful with the conversion attempt he landed a further penalty goal and despite Keighley's late try the Challenge Cup was returning to Lancashire.

1937 RUGBY LEAGUE CHALLENGE CUP FINAL
Saturday 8 May 1937, Wembley Stadium, London

	T	G	P		T	G	P
KEIGHLEY	1	1	5	**WIDNES**	4	3	18
I. Herbert				W. Bradley			
R. Sherburn		1		F. Whyte			
I. A. Towill				P. Topping		3	
G. Parker				K. Barber	1		
R. Lloyd	1			T. Evans			
L. Bevan				T. Shannon	1		
D. Davies				T. McCue	1		
J. Traill				N. Silcock Capt	1		
C. Halliday				J. Jones			
H. Jones				A. Higgins			
E. Dixon				H. McDowell			
F. Talbot				R. Roberts			
J. Gill				H. Millington			

Referee: P. Cowell (Warrington)
Half Time: 8-0; Attendance: 47,699

Below: Nat Silcock carries the Challenge Cup around Wembley Stadium

The Homecoming

On the Monday after the Final the reception from Widnes fans outstripped anything previously experienced.

Following their arrival at Runcorn Station the players boarded an open top coach with the Cup and took a roundabout route, led by the Widnes Subscription Band, through Runcorn before arriving at the Transporter.

As they arrived at the bridge, which was decorated in black and white, the crowds in West Bank were clearly visible. Once back in Widnes the players boarded a lorry and the Nazareth House Band joined the procession.

As it passed through West Bank banners proclaimed "A Gradely Welcome", "We're Proud Of You", "Welcome to the Victors" and "Well done Widnes; Welcome Home"

The scene in the Town Hall Square was amazing as a detachment of mounted police led the players through the town. The players, led by the Mayor and Mayoress climbed onto a specially constructed platform with the Mayor welcoming " our victorious boys home again".

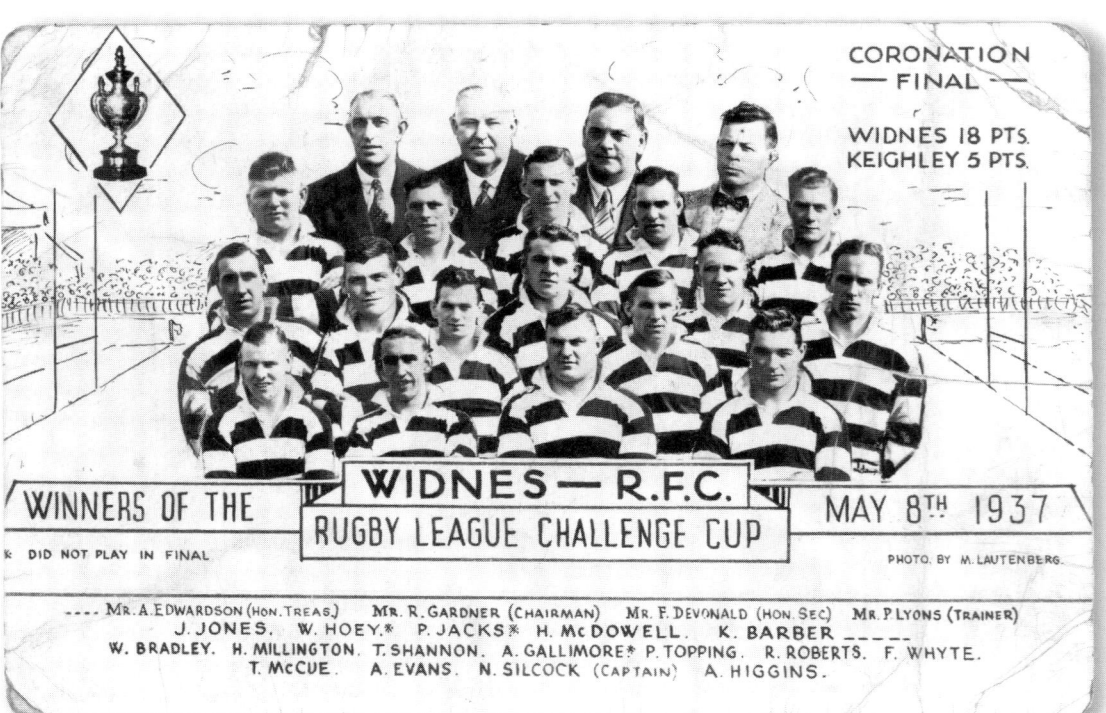

CORONATION FINAL
WIDNES 18 PTS.
KEIGHLEY 5 PTS.

WINNERS OF THE RUGBY LEAGUE CHALLENGE CUP — WIDNES — R.F.C. — MAY 8TH 1937

* DID NOT PLAY IN FINAL   PHOTO. BY M. LAUTENBERG.

---- Mr. A. EDWARDSON (HON. TREAS.)   MR. R. GARDNER (CHAIRMAN)   MR. F. DEVONALD (HON. SEC)   MR. P. LYONS (TRAINER)
J. JONES.   W. HOEY.*   P. JACKS*   H. McDOWELL.   K. BARBER _____
W. BRADLEY.   H. MILLINGTON.   T. SHANNON.   A. GALLIMORE*   P. TOPPING.   R. ROBERTS.   F. WHYTE.
T. McCUE.   A. EVANS.   N. SILCOCK (CAPTAIN)   A. HIGGINS.

*Victorious...
Nat Silcock becomes the second Widnes captain to raise the famous trophy at Wembley Stadium*

Right & Below: Widnes players, with trainer Peter Lyons, prepare for the 1937 Wembley Final

Captain Nat Silcock said they were very pleased with the great welcome. Three years ago they had said they would do their best to bring the Cup back and they had done so.

'Now here is the Cup and here are the kids who have done it. They are a good set of boys; they are very sturdy, clean living and willing to do anything I ask them and that is everything in a team. We are not beauties, we were not born like this, we have had a bit of knocking about.'

1950 RUGBY LEAGUE CHALLENGE CUP FINAL
WARRINGTON V WIDNES
Saturday 6 May 1950, Wembley Stadium, London

1950 The Road to Wembley

The 1950 Challenge Cup competition saw the first round played over two legs. Widnes were drawn against Rochdale Hornets and in the first leg at Naughton Park the Chemics ran out winners by 15-2.

Taking a 13 point advantage into the second leg Widnes made easy work of the Rochdale side and a 27-0 victory on the day gave them an overall win of 42-2.

The second round was a much more even contest as Widnes travelled to Batley where they won 12-4 before a home victory over Barrow in the Quarter Finals by 12-7.

The Semi-Final this time was played at Central Park, Wigan where the Chemics defeated Bradford Northern by 8-0 in front of a crowd of just under 25,000.

This set up a 'derby' Challenge Cup Final with Warrington who had defeated Leeds in the Semi-Final by 16-4 in front of a crowd of over 70,000 at Odsal Stadium, Bradford.

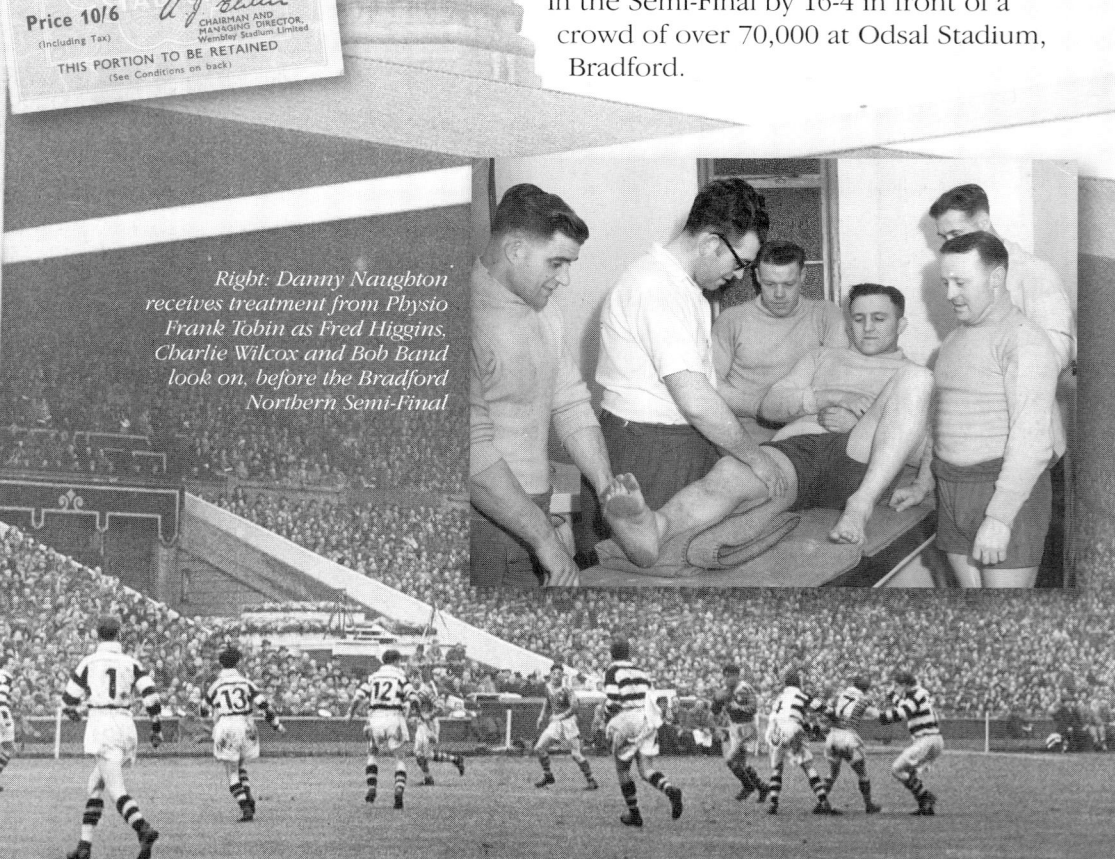

Right: Danny Naughton receives treatment from Physio Frank Tobin as Fred Higgins, Charlie Wilcox and Bob Band look on, before the Bradford Northern Semi-Final

Warrington reached the Semi-Final stage by defeating Hull KR in the two-legged first round, 12-2 away and 24-4 at Wilderspool. In the second round they defeated Swinton 17-2 at Wilderspool and a home draw in the Quarter Final saw them account for Hunslet 12-7.

The Game

The town of Widnes give the team a magnificent send off. Crowds gathered at the Town Hall square and the traffic was almost at a standstill in the town of Widnes. The players were travelling by coach taking them to Liverpool for the London train. It was expected that there would be 90,000 spectators at the stadium and 21,000 of them would be from Widnes.

Above: Tommy Sale goes over for a try for Widnes in their Semi-Final victory over Bradford Northern

Widnes were to be handicapped in the Final as two of their star players, Danny Naughton and Fred Higgins, had been selected for the Great Britain tour to Australia which departed before the Final.

Above: Prime Minister Clement Atlee shakes hands with Bob Band (hooker) as he is introduced to the Widnes players before the 1950 Final

It was to be Warrington's first victory for 43 years to win the Challenge Cup and it was a well deserved one, Warrington were the better team and outplayed a poor Widnes side. Warrington were more alert, faster and fitter than Widnes. The first points were scored for Warrington in the 16th minute by Palin, who dropped a goal from loose play in front of the Widnes posts. Then 2 minutes later Palin added another 2 points with a tremendous touchline penalty kick. Before Widnes had time to compose themselves Harry Bath the Australian loose forward crossed the Chemics' line for a try and Palin converted, another 5 points for Warrington.

Above: The scrum collapses in the 1950 Final

Below: The Widnes defence repels yet another Warrington attack

Widnes players Ron Rowbottom and Fred Leigh played some fine Rugby League but the players let themselves down by dropping the ball and fumbling passes. By mistakes Widnes made before half time Warrington scored another 5 points, the try was by Ron Ryder and the penalty kick was by Palin.

The Chemics came out a stronger team in the second half and held Warrington firm for 22 minutes in the second half but then another penalty goal by Palin increased the lead to 16-0.

With 13 minutes to go Warrington scored a classic Wembley try by Knowelden. It was the final score of the match.

Warrington had beaten Widnes 19-0 and the Lance Todd Trophy winner was Gerry Helme of Warrington. The captain Harry Bath was carried shoulder high around Wembley Stadium showing off the Challenge Cup to the fans.

Widnes were left feeling disappointed and sorry for their fans that had travelled down to London to support them. But on the day Warrington were the better team.

Peter Spencer was a disappointed fan that day, "Gerry Helme won the man of the match award before a ball was kicked that day. Widnes played Titch Anderson opposite him and when the team emerged from the dressing rooms, Anderson was covered in bandages. I don't know how he could bend his left leg!

"After the game we had a walk round London again and people were asking us who had won. We told them it was Warrington but they didn't believe us 'cos the Warrington fans looked so miserable!"

Above: Captain Tommy Sale leads out the Widnes team for the 1950 Challenge Cup Final at Wembley Stadium

1950 RUGBY LEAGUE CHALLENGE CUP FINAL
Saturday 6 May 1950, Wembley Stadium, London

	T	G	P		T	G	P
WARRINGTON	**3**	**5**	**19**	**WIDNES**	**0**	**0**	**0**
L. Jones				F. Bradley			
B. Bevan				J. Parkes			
R. Ryder	1			C. Hutton			
A. Naughton				T. Sale Capt			
A. Johnson				A. Malone			
B. Knowelden	1			J. Fleming			
G. Helme				H. Anderson			
W. Derbyshire				R. Rowbottom			
H. Fishwick				R. Band			
H. Fisher				C. Wilcox			
H. Bath	1			F. Leigh			
G. Lowe				J. Naughton			
H. Palin		5		C. Reynolds			

Referee: A. Dobson (Pontefract)
Half Time: 14-0; Attendance: 94,249

The Homecoming

Despite losing to Warrington four coach loads of members of the Widnes Supporters Club greeted the team as the train from London pulled into Liverpool Lime Street on the Monday evening following the game.

The fans crowded round the team waving rattles and bunting as the players walked to the coach waiting to take them back to Widnes. The Mayor and Mayoress, who had travelled with the party, returned to Widnes by car to be back in time for the civic reception.

The four coaches followed the team coach whilst three motor cycles carrying fans wearing black and white joined the procession and led the players' coach.

At Childwall Valley Road a police car joined the party and led the convoy for the rest of the journey to Widnes.

The players waved from the roof of the coach as it approached Widnes as people lined the streets and sat at upstairs windows of houses, waving flags and rattles.

Below: The official 1950 Wembley party at the premises of Phillips (Electrical) at Shaftsbury Street

Above: The 1950 Widnes Challenge Cup team

Below right: Fred Higgins and Danny Naughton were sorely missed by Widnes in the 1950 Challenge Cup Final

The band of St Aidan's Cadets and the Widnes Subscription Band joined the parade as it reached Deacon Road and they took it in turns to play as the coach moved at walking pace through a channel of policemen.

Earlier in the afternoon there had been open-air tea parties for the town's children and they were amongst the first to make their way to the Town Hall square. By seven o'clock there were thousands of fans in position and vehicles had to be diverted away from the town centre.

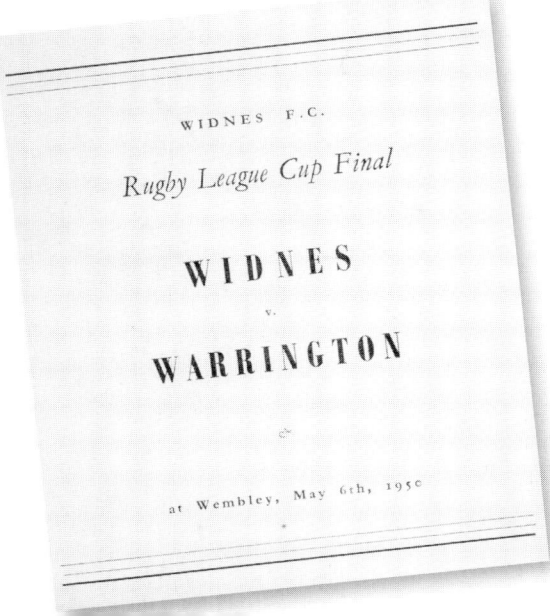

THE RUGBY LEAGUE CHALLENGE CUP COMPETITION

FINAL TIE

HULL KINGSTON ROVERS
v
WIDNES

SATURDAY, MAY 9th 1964   Kick-off 3 p.m.

EMPIRE STADIUM

OFFICIAL PROGRAMME · · · ONE SHILLING

**1964 RUGBY LEAGUE CHALLENGE CUP FINAL
HULL KR V WIDNES**
Saturday 9 May 1964, Wembley Stadium, London

1964 The Road to Wembley

The Luck of the Draw...

Widnes went through a year you could possibly call irritating, nerve racking but most of all exciting. Widnes showed courage and strength going through replay after replay.

In the first round they went head to head with Leigh at Hilton Park where they drew 3-3. In the replay at Naughton Park the teams drew 11-11 and so a second replay was held at Knowsley Road, St Helens where Widnes grabbed the opportunity of snatching a win over Leigh 14-2.

In the second round the Chemics clashed in a local derby with Liverpool City the visitors, Widnes winning 16-6. For the Quarter Finals Widnes were drawn at home again, this time against Swinton. The match ended in a 5-5 draw and so the teams met again at Station Road where after 80 minutes they played out a 0-0 draw.

The second Quarter Final replay was scheduled for Central Park, Wigan and it gave way to an emphatic Widnes victory, 15-3.

Widnes returned to Station Road, Swinton for their Semi-Final against Castleford and once again there was no separating the teams as they fought out a 7-7 draw before a crowd of over 25,000. The Semi-Final replay was held at Belle Vue, Wakefield and this time over 28,500 fans saw Widnes edge out Castleford 7-5 to reach their first Final in 14 years.

Their opponents in the Final Hull Kingston Rovers, also had to go through replays on the way to their first ever Wembley appearance.

In the first round they drew at home 12-12 to Rochdale Hornets before comfortably winning the

Left: 'On your marks' Jim Measures, Alan Briers, Ged Lowe, Bobby Chisnall and Johnny Gaydon are ready to come out of the traps on a visit to Wembley Stadium prior to the big day. Wally Hurstfield looks on as Edgar Bate puts the players under starters orders.

replay 22-7. An easy second round victory at York, 23-7, led to a home Quarter Final tie against Barrow and an equally convincing 38-4 victory. In the Semi-Final they took on Oldham at Headingley Stadium in Leeds and over 28,500 fans saw the teams play out a 5-5 draw.

The replay was held at Station Road, Swinton and 12 minutes into extra time the game was abandoned due to bad light with Oldham leading 17-14. The second replay took place at Huddersfield's Fartown ground and Hull KR emerged victorious by 12-2. Nearly 33,000 fans watched this encounter and with over 27,000 at the first replay this tie was witnessed by over 88,000 people, more than attended the actual Final!

A Year never to be forgotten, 1964 the year of the draws, the question on everybodies' lips was 'Would Widnes draw again in the Final?'

Widnes' Frank Myler, cousin of Vince Karalius, remembers the build up to the Final. "The town was great in the lead up to the game. All the shops were decorated in black and white and all the talk was of the match."

The Game

Despite this being their first time at Wembley, Hull Kingston Rovers were installed as pre-match favourites but on the day the Widnes side was far more superior than their East Coast rivals.

Despite this obvious superiority the Widnes side struggled to find a way through their opponents defence and the only points of the first forty minutes came via the boot of full back Bob Randall who kicked a penalty goal five minutes before the break when Rovers were penalised for 'foot up' in the scrum.

Right: 'Man of the Match' Frank Collier goes over for a crucial try to sink the hopes of Hull Kingston Rovers

Widnes went in for their first try on 52 minutes when Jim Measures sent Ray Owen away. Although the scrum half was tackled short, from the resultant play the ball Vince Karalius put centre Alan Briers in for a try.

Above: Centre Alan Briers miraculously stays in play leaving the Rovers defence in tatters to score

Left: Frank Myler celebrates with Ray Owen after scoring a long range try at Wembley

Within five minutes Widnes had extended their lead as Wally Hurstfield and Arthur Hughes combined to send Frank Myler over and with Randall converting one of these tries the Chemics led 10-0.

Although Hull Kingston Rovers pulled 5 points back with a try from Burwell converted by Kellett, Widnes had the final say when man-of-the match Frank Collier touched down in the 78th minute.

Above: 'Cousins in Arms...' Vince Karalius and Frank Myler collect the silverware as delighted Chairman Frank Devonald looks on

The evening reception was at the Waldorf Hotel but the players, wives and officials to their credit left their banquet to take the Cup to Euston Station where Widnes fans were waiting to catch the midnight train home.

Myler continued, "To play and win for your home town at Wembley was a dream come true. It was the greatest honour of my career." (This from a man who captained the GB team to an Ashes victory in Australia, a feat not repeated since).

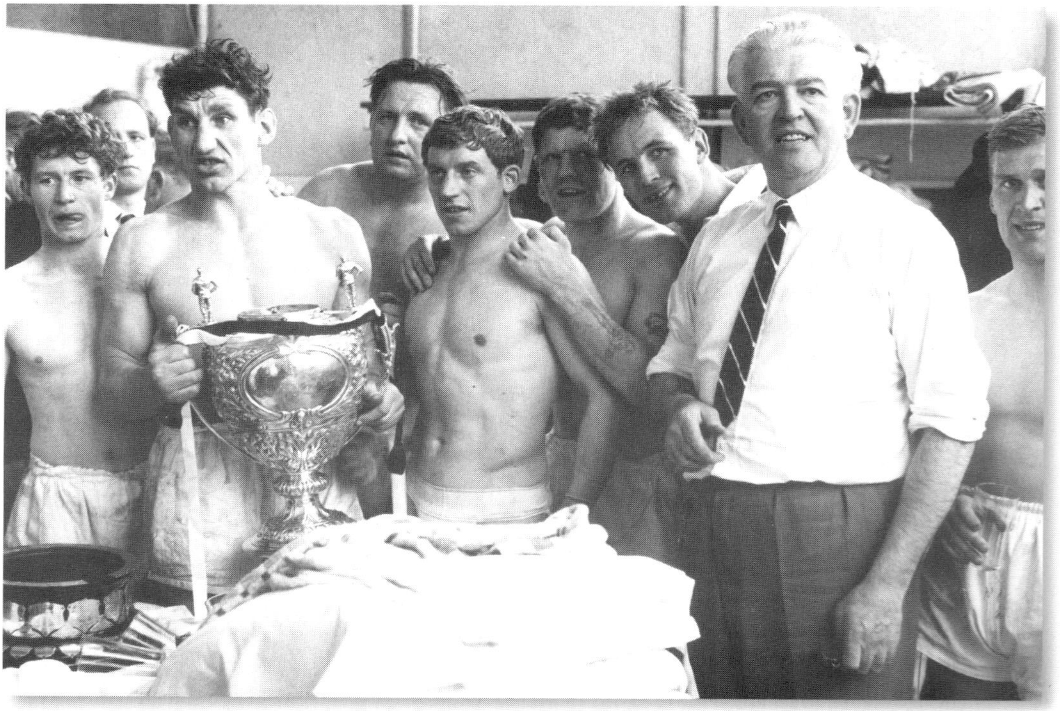

1964 RUGBY LEAGUE CHALLENGE CUP FINAL
Saturday 9 May 1964, Wembley Stadium, London

HULL KR	T	G	P	WIDNES	T	G	P
	1	1	5		3	2	13
C. Kellett		1		R. Randall		2	
G. Paul				R. Chisnall			
T. Major				A. Briers	1		
D. Elliott				F. Myler	1		
M. Blackmore				W. Thompson			
A. Burwell	1			G. Lowe			
A. Bunting				R. Owen			
B. Tyson				W. Hurstfield			
P. Flanagan				G. Kemel			
B. Mennell				F. Collier	1		
E. Palmer				J. Measures			
L. Clark				A. Hughes			
H. Poole				V. Karalius Capt			

Referee: R Thomas (Oldham)
Half Time: 0-2; Attendance: 84,488

Below: Widnes captain Vince Karalius lifts the 1964 Challenge Cup surrounded by his team-mates

The Homecoming

15,000 proud Widnesians gathered in Victoria Square to welcome back the Cup Winners, swaying and surging forward on a sea of black and white all with the same thought, to catch a glimpse of the town's all-conquering heroes.

As the team coach pulled onto the Town Hall forecourt 'March of the Gladiators' was played but it was lost in the tumultuous welcome, thunderous applause and cheering as Vince Karalius held the Cup high above the heads of his team mates on the open top bus.

The crowds had been very patient as the players were an hour and a quarter behind schedule but they would have waited all night for this moment.

The bus had made its way via Runcorn and the team and officials looked flabbergasted at the crowd scenes at the new bridge spur road and traffic island which were likened only in size to those when Princess Alexandra opened the bridge three years earlier.

It had been estimated that 2,000 Runcornians had made the trip to Wembley and there was double that number waiting for the team to arrive with the Heath Road slipway blocked by fans. As the team crossed the bridge two boys ran parallel with the coach along the top-most girders of the old railway bridge.

As the party arrived in West Bank, supporters decked in black and white lined the route with children sat on their father's shoulders to see an occasion they would not easily forget.

Having reached Victoria Square they received a fantastic reception with champagne flowing and Karalius and Frank Collier handing it round on the platform. Every time Karalius lifted the Cup, more than a dozen times, there was a resounding cheer from the crowd.

Following speeches from the Mayor and Alderman Swale, the Widnes captain Karalius took the microphone, "I thank you very much for giving us a great welcome. I cannot say how much it means to us. Thanks a lot for coming and thanks for all the support."

The team then set off on a 20 mile lap of honour with thousands following the bus until it reached Lowerhouse Lane. Once at the clubhouse another fantastic reception awaited them and the crowd was such that Lowerhouse Lane was blocked completely and police had to link arms to make a passage from the coach to the players' entrance for the team.

Once inside the calm and quiet of the club the players, their wives and girlfriends and Naughton Park officials settled back for a welcome cup of tea and refreshments.

THE RUGBY LEAGUE CHALLENGE CUP COMPETITION

FINAL

SATURDAY, 10 MAY, 1975

WARRINGTON

versus

WIDNES

OFFICIAL PROGRAMME
FIFTEEN PENCE

WEMBLEY STADIUM

KICK OFF
3 p.m.

**1975 RUGBY LEAGUE CHALLENGE CUP FINAL
WARRINGTON V WIDNES**
Saturday 10 May 1975, Wembley Stadium, London

1975 The Road to Wembley

Despite the success in the early rounds of the Challenge Cup Widnes fans probably weren't too pleased because not one of the games was drawn at home.

Round one produced a tie at Swinton which Widnes won 13-4, Chris Anderson, Keith Elwell and John Peek the try scorers and Ray Dutton scoring two conversions.

In the second round Widnes scored a narrow victory at Hull ending 13-12. Mal Aspey and Mick George the try scorers, Dutton with 3 conversions and Mick Adams dropping a goal. This victory meant that Widnes went back in to the hat and were drawn at Oldham in the Quarter Final.

The Chemics prevailed 10-4 Mick Adams the only try scorer for Widnes, Dutton adding 3 goals and Ashton with a drop goal giving Widnes a place in the last four.

The Semi Final was at Odsal Stadium, Bradford with the opponents Wakefield Trinity. The final score on the day was 13-7. Doug Laughton and John Foran going over for the tries while Ray Dutton added 3 goals and a drop goal.

WIDNES SEMI-FINAL ACTION!

5 April — Odsal, Bradford
Wakefield Trinity   7pts
Widnes   13pts

Widnes skipper, Doug Laughton, dives through to score the first try against Wakefield Trinity.

The confidence in the side had been constantly building with every victory in every game. Loose forward and captain Doug Laughton commented, "We felt like we couldn't get beat. We genuinely believed that we were unbeatable. It could be compared with the Australian Kangaroos now; they don't get beat because they don't think they can." This may have been due to coach Vince Karalius. Former Widnes player and Australian coach Chris Anderson said "Vince instilled a great team spirit and a great

The try which clinched the semi-final. Forward John Foran dives over to score in the last few minutes.

No doubt which dressing room! It is, of course, jubilant Widnes after their great semi-final win.

belief. Before the Final I genuinely believed we were going to win which is unusual for such a big game."

The Chemics opponents in the Final were to be close rivals and current holders Warrington. In 1950 Warrington had defeated Widnes 19-0 in the Final, so revenge was certainly on everybodies' mind.

Warrington defeated Halifax 32-6 at Wilderspool Stadium in the first round and then in a local derby travelled to Central Park, Wigan where they defeated the home side 24-17.

In the Quarter Finals the Primrose and Blue side travelled over the Pennines to Leeds where they took on, and beat, New Hunslet 23-3.

This earnt them a Semi-Final spot against Leeds and a return to the site of their second round victory, this time defeating Leeds 11-4 in front of a crowd of over 13,000.

Above: Chris Anderson who was flown over from Australia especially for the Cup Final

BACK ROW *(left to right)* : M. George, M. Aspey, R. Dutton, J. Mills, J. Foran, M. Adams, N. Nelson, J. Wood. FRONT ROW : E. Hughes, A. Prescott, K. Elwell, D. Laughton (Capt), R. Bowden, T. Karalius, J. O'Neill

Right: Action from the 1975 Challenge Cup Final... Mal Aspey, Keith Elwell and Chris Anderson try to keep Doug Laughton in play

Below: Widnes Coach Vince Karalius in thoughtful pose on the bench at Wembley with Ged Lowe (left), Harry Dawson (right) and Jimmy O'Neill (foreground)

Widnes fullback that year was Ray Dutton. "We'd had a couple of easy games in the opening rounds but the further we got the harder it got although we were very confident going into the Semi-Final.

"The atmosphere in the town was electric building up to the Final, everywhere you went people wanted to talk to you. I've never known anything like it.

"We travelled down to Wembley on the Thursday and the next morning were due to go to the Stadium to have a look around. As we were waiting in the hotel car park Reg Bowden found a dead rat so he thought it would be a good idea to plant it across the steering wheel on the coach whilst the driver, Barry Hynan, had nipped to the toilet. When he came back and sat at the wheel this rat was just sat there 'staring' at him!

The Game

A Challenge Cup Final is a big thing in a town like Widnes with a rich Rugby League heritage. Special trains ran from Ditton which resulted in a massive gathering of people at the station.

Black and white top hats with Widnes RLFC splashed across were worn proudly as were black and white Widnes rosettes which, if you peeled the sticker off, actually turned out to be Fulham FC rosettes from the FA Cup Final against West Ham the same year!

It was a special occasion for Widnes fan Brian Clarke who, along with David Hulme, played in the u11's curtain raiser before the game. He said "It was an unbelievable time for me. It was the first schoolboy curtain raiser at the Final and I remember the town team coach Mr Kennedy telling us all and we couldn't believe it. We became minor celebrities up to and, for a while, after the Final. I remember walking onto the Wembley turf and there was about 40 000 in the ground at the time and my legs were like jelly."

Below: Mick Adams draws the Warrington defence as Kevin Ashcroft, Mal Aspey, John Foran and Barry Sheridan look on

Right: Widnes try scorer Jim Mills takes on the Warrington defence

In the tunnel before the game there were a few mind games and intimidatory comments made by both sides. One in particular was the Warrington players calling Widnes the 'Coca Cola boys' because of the booze ban imposed by the coaching staff. This turned out be beneficial however as Widnes' fitness levels played a key role in securing the 14-7 defeat over arch rivals Warrington.

The atmosphere at Wembley has been described by many legendary sportsmen as second to none. Chris Anderson backed this claim up, "As you step on to the pitch the atmosphere hits you. The full house singing. I've never heard that before. It's something that stays with you for your whole career, it was my first real big occasion in rugby league and I'll never forget the atmosphere."

Another famous part of Wembley is the supposedly 'tiring effect' the pitch has upon your legs and the fatigue is much greater at Wembley. Widnes prepared for this by going to a similar pitch in Southport for training. All of this preparation and all of the confidence coach Karalius had instilled in the players paid off.

In the Final on 10th May 1975, Widnes beat Warrington 14-7. Jim Mills scored Widnes' only try, "It was my first Wembley appearance so it was very special to score a try on my debut at the stadium."

Ray Dutton kicked 5 goals and 1 drop goal and deservedly picked up the Lance Todd trophy. "I was just relieved that the game was over and we had won."

Widnes went 5 points behind after just 5 minutes when John Bevan crossed to give the 'Wires' an early lead. Warrington, however couldn't make it last and Widnes were dominant for the remaining 75 minutes.

Dutton missed his first penalty attempt from 40 yards after Ashcroft was penalised for a foul on Keith Elwell. Minutes later Alan Whittle was caught offside in the same spot, Dutton didn't miss with his second attempt. Eric Hughes came close to a try but was pushed into the corner flag by Warrington full back Whitehead.

Mick Adams was also unlucky when he was tripped by Whitehead after chipping the ball over the full back. Widnes were awarded the penalty and Dutton was on hand to add two points to the scoreboard in favour of Widnes.

After a lot of Widnes pressure Jim Mills went over and this try effectively settled the game. Dutton landed the conversion to take his tally to three goals for the afternoon. Just before half time Dutton scored another penalty goal making it 11-5 to Widnes at the break.

Three minutes after the interval Derek Whitehead converted a penalty into two points but it wasn't enough to revive the tiring Warrington side. Dutton scored a drop goal and then a penalty goal before full time making the Final score Widnes 14 Warrington 7.

Widnes had imposed a massive upset beating favourites Warrington. Warrington coach Alex Murphy could only reply, "Things do go wrong sometimes. The Titanic sank."

"After such a big game and such a big build up your initial reaction is just relief that it's over and you've won. After a while what you've achieved does start to sink in but immediately after the final whistle it's sheer relief." Anderson reflected.

For Doug Laughton, winning the Challenge Cup was a dream come true, "Since I was about 9 years old I said to myself 'one day I'll win the Challenge Cup' and I had, all I wanted to do was lift the Cup."

The 1975 Challenge Cup Final was won by the underdogs Widnes and some say it sparked the revival of 'The Cup Kings.' It had been over 10 years since Widnes had been to Wembley but for many it was worth the wait. Widnes had repaid Warrington the defeat at Wembley from 1950.

Ray Dutton had played an outstanding game and was rewarded with the Lance Todd trophy for man of the match. "The main thing was that we had won the Cup, to be given the man of the match award was just an added bonus.

"As soon as the final whistle went I went over to where my mam was 'cos I knew she'd be crying. Then we went up for the Cup and on a lap of honour and I didn't know I'd won the Lance Todd Trophy until I was interviewed by Grandstand's Frank Bough.

"I was absolutely elated and also felt very humble as there had been some great players who'd won the trophy and now my name was going to be on there. I felt 10 feet tall, it was the pinnacle of my career, especially as we had beaten Warrington, our fiercest rivals."

1975 RUGBY LEAGUE CHALLENGE CUP FINAL
Saturday 10 May 1975, Wembley Stadium, London

WARRINGTON	T	G	P	WIDNES	T	G	P
	1	2	7		1	6	14
D. Whitehead		2		R. Dutton		6	
M. Philbin				A. Prescott			
D. Noonan				M. George			
F. Reynolds				M. Aspey			
J. Bevan	1			C. Anderson			
A. Whittle				E. Hughes			
P. Gordon				R. Bowden			
D. Chisnall				J. Mills	1		
K. Ashcroft				K. Elwell			
B. Wanbon				B. Sheridan			
T. Conroy				J. Foran			
T. Martyn				M. Adams			
B. Philbin				D. Laughton Capt			
W. Briggs				Jim O'Neill			
M. Nicholas				N. Nelson			

Referee: P Geraghty (York)
Half Time: 5-11; Attendance: 85,098

The Homecoming

It looked as though all Widnes was crowded round the Municipal Building ready to welcome home their heroes on the day after the Final.

Over 20,000 people gathered in Widnes town centre and a massive shout went up when the loudspeakers announced the returning Chemics had been seen on the outskirts of the town.

Then the countdown began… they had reached Birchfield Road, Kingsway, each sighting faithfully relayed over the public address system until a crescendo of cheers, whistles and tooting car horns announced that the team had arrived.

Coach Vince Karalius held aloft by Jim Mills with the coveted Challenge Cup outside the Municipal Building

Onto the balcony, followed by his team-mates, strode captain Doug Laughton clutching the Challenge Cup. Glinting in the sunlight the trophy was lifted high into the air greeted by a deafening chorus of triumph.

The crowd became a sea of black and white as row upon row of Chemics scarves, rosettes, flags and banners swayed back and forth.

When coach Vince Karalius appeared the crowd roared their approval as, hoisted onto the shoulders of his team, he once again savoured the unique taste of champagne drunk from the Challenge Cup.

Below: Try scorer Jim Mills shows off the silverware to the fans

THE RUGBY LEAGUE CHALLENGE CUP COMPETITION

FINAL

SATURDAY, 8 MAY, 1976

ST. HELENS

VERSUS

WIDNES

OFFICIAL PROGRAMME TWENTY PENCE

WEMBLEY STADIUM

KICK OFF 3 p.m.

**1976 RUGBY LEAGUE CHALLENGE CUP FINAL
ST HELENS V WIDNES**
Saturday 8 May 1976, Wembley Stadium, London

1976 The Road to Wembley

The Chemics' defence of the Challenge Cup started at Naughton Park where they defeated Batley 26-4. Their reward was another home draw, this time Wigan were the visitors and Widnes recorded a 7-5 victory to move into the Quarter Finals.

For this game they travelled to Wilderspool to take on a Warrington side looking to avenge their Cup Final defeat 12 months earlier but it was the Black and Whites who claimed victory by 6-0.

In the Semi-Finals Widnes were drawn against Yorkshire side Featherstone Rovers and in a thrilling game at Swinton's Station Road ground, 13,000 fans saw the Chemics come from 9-0 down to take the game 15-9 and book their place in the second successive Final.

Their opponents were to be near neighbours St Helens who had begun their path to Wembley on Humberside where, in a close encounter, they beat Hull 5-3 at the Boulevard.

They were a little closer to home in the second round taking on Salford at The Willows and running out victors by 17-11 which gave them a home Quarter Final tie against Oldham and a 17-9 victory put them through to the Semi-Finals

The Saints took on Keighley at Fartown, Huddersfield for a place in the Cup Final and won through by the narrowest margin, 5-4 to take their place at Wembley.

WIDNES SEMI-FINAL ACTION!

2nd April—Headingley, Leeds
Hull Kingston Rvrs. . . 5pts
Widnes 14pts

Ray Dutton, 29-year-old full back, scored 14 goals during Widnes' Cup run to Wembley.

Here's Stuart Wright in full flight hotly pursued by Dick Wallace (No. 1) and Clive Sullivan (No. 5) scored a semi-final try.

Doug Laughton, 14 stone, 31-year-old loose forward finds the going tough as four Hull K.R. players check his progress. Laughton is making his fourth Wembley Cup Final appearance today.

The Game

"In 1976 there was a lot more pressure than in 1975" said Ray Dutton. "I guess that's how Warrington felt in 1975 having won the Challenge Cup in 1974."

After weeks of preparation, the day of the Final had arrived. Wembley Stadium was filling swiftly as eager fans poured in. The atmosphere was ecstatic. The whole crowd was cheering and chanting.

"The pressure was on, even more than the year before as we had great performances to live up to from the past years. It was baking hot and humid," said Doug Laughton, so it made it even more challenging for the players to get on the pitch and play well. However this wasn't so different from the previous year because "It was just a matter of turning up and playing your best", says Ray Dutton.

Finally all of the players were lined up in the tunnel." The two teams were stood side by side. Ray Dutton said, "I couldn't describe the feeling of waiting in the tunnel." The first whistle blew and the game kicked off.

Above: Mark Dutton and his Chemics teddy get a lift from father Ray

Below: Widnes prop John Wood on the charge

Above: Eddie Cunningham of St Helens evades the tackle of John Wood

After the first 13 minutes Saints' Eddie Cunningham scored and the try was converted to make the score 5-0.

Dutton landed two penalty goals either side of a Pimblett drop goal to give an interval scoreline of 6-4 in favour of St Helens.

The scoring in the second half began with a drop goal by Keith Ellwell for Widnes making the score 6-5 to Saints. On sixty-seven minutes Geoff Pimblett yet again scored but this time with a drop goal. One minute later, a try from Heaton converted by Pimblett won the match for St Helens.

Two more tries from substitute Peter Glynn, a Widnesian, one of which was converted completed the scoring. The final whistle blew and the overall score was 20-5 to St Helens. The dream of becoming Wembley champions twice in a row was over.

The man of the match was Geoff Pimblett. Widnes went home empty handed because of this big disappointment at Wembley.

The players were to have people on their backs all week, so John Foran told us. They wouldn't have been paid a lot either because at that time if you lost a match you were paid a lot less than you would have been if you had won.

The only success that did come from this campaign was when "Eric Hughes bet five hundred pounds on Red Rum in The Grand National on the day of the Semi Final and won seven thousand pounds," John Foran recalled.

Doug Laughton had his own thoughts on the game, when asked whether he thought that the team had the upper hand at any time in the match, he simply replied with "No".

He then followed that with an honest opinion, which was that he thought "We had done everything wrong in the season. We knew the opposing team were a lot older than us so most would assume we had the better chance of winning."

We also asked Doug if he had any superstitions during his career. He told us that he had his fortune told once but other than that he said he didn't have any.

We were also interested to know about how he felt once the terrible trial was over. He said, "I was embarrassed." This was the kind of reaction we were expecting from someone who was there during this "awful performance". But even though losing at Wembley was bad, Doug said that drawing at Wembley would have been worse. It was truly one of the worst games Widnes have ever played and to do it at Wembley was utterly "humiliating".

Thankfully the reaction at home wasn't half as bad as Doug's. Even though he confessed "it was a fair game, people at home argued it wasn't and that the hot weather put us off gaining our deserved title of Wembley Champions. We were sometimes a bit too overconfident", but again he admitted he didn't think we'd win. He revealed that "we went into the match with a bad attitude."

"There wasn't the same intensity as in the previous year" added Dutton. "A lot of us thought we just had to turn up and go through the moves. By the time we realized we had to do something different it was too late. Saints ground us down and paced themselves for the full eighty minutes. The best part of the game was the final whistle."

Another debutant in 1976 was mascot Paul Hansbury who is now the equipment manager at the Club.

"I was only 8 at the time and used to come down and watch training all the time. After one session Mick Adams came and asked me if I wanted to be mascot... he didn't have to ask twice! At the time they didn't have mascots so my mum and dad took me down to Wembley and as the kit was unloaded I went in! I remember the game well although I was very nervous as there was a massive crowd there. I also met Margaret Thatcher!

1976 RUGBY LEAGUE CHALLENGE CUP FINAL
Saturday 8 May 1976, Wembley Stadium, London

ST HELENS	T 4	G 5	P 20	WIDNES	T 0	G 3	P 5
G. Pimblett		5		R. Dutton		2	
L. Jones				A. Prescott			
E. Cunningham	1			E. Hughes			
D. Noonan				M. George			
R. Mathias				D. Jenkins			
W. Benyon				D. Eckersley			
J. Heaton	1			R. Bowden Capt			
J. Mantle				N. Nelson			
A. Karalius				K. Elwell		1	
K. Coslett				J. Wood			
G. Nicholls				J. Foran			
E. Chisnall				M. Adams			
D. Hull				D. Laughton			
Subs				*Subs*			
P. Glynn		2		D. O'Neill			
M. James				B. Sheridan			

Referee: R Moore (Wakefield)
Half Time: 6-4; Attendance: 89,982

The Homecoming

In a fantastic show of loyalty thousands of supporters gathered on the fields outside the Municipal Building on the Sunday evening following the game and turned defeat into victory, disappointment into delight.

Left: 'Behind enemy lines...' Widnesians George Nicholls, Tony Karalius and Peter Glynn celebrate a victory over their home town team

The fans started to arrive with their banners and their songs as early as 1pm and soon the centre of Widnes was alive and buzzing in a sea of black and white. Everyone, it seemed, had bought new trousers, new jumpers, new hats, new everything - and all in their favourite team's colours. No-one was going to be miserable!

Children sat on the central reservation in Kingsway chanting 'Wid-nes Wid-nes' others paraded majestically in their huge top hats and painted banners which they had draped around their shoulders. Young couples walked hand in hand, stopping at the hot-dog stands while pensioners enjoyed the sunny Spring evening with a cooling ice-lolly.

Such was the happy, relaxed, almost carnival atmosphere generated by the fans that it was hard to imagine that 'Myler's Bionic Soldiers' were not actually bringing the Challenge Cup with them. Even the Cheshire Police Band captured the mood and played 'Congratulations' over and over again.

When the team arrived in their open-topped double decker bus over an hour late - their coach had broken down - there was such a deafening roar from the swaying mass that a flock of pigeons flew off the library roof in fright!

At 6.35pm, led by the Mayor of Halton, the immaculately brown-suited Widnes contingent made its way up the fancy black and white platform to receive the adulation of the faithful.

"Three cheers for the lads" shouted the Mayor, Cllr Charles Helsby but there was no need for prompting. From the moment the team appeared to the moment they set off on their 15 mile tour of Widnes and Runcorn, the cheers rang out, very clear and very loud.

In fact the only time there was a hush was when Frank Myler came forward to speak. Obviously choked by the great reception there was only one thing he could say to the fans who worshipped him and his team, and he said it. "There's another year next year."

Perhaps the people who summed it up best were two little girls who spent that Sunday afternoon making their own banner. Draped over one of the crash barriers at the front it said, "The future's not hard to see, you'll go back to Wem-b-ley, 77." How right they were!

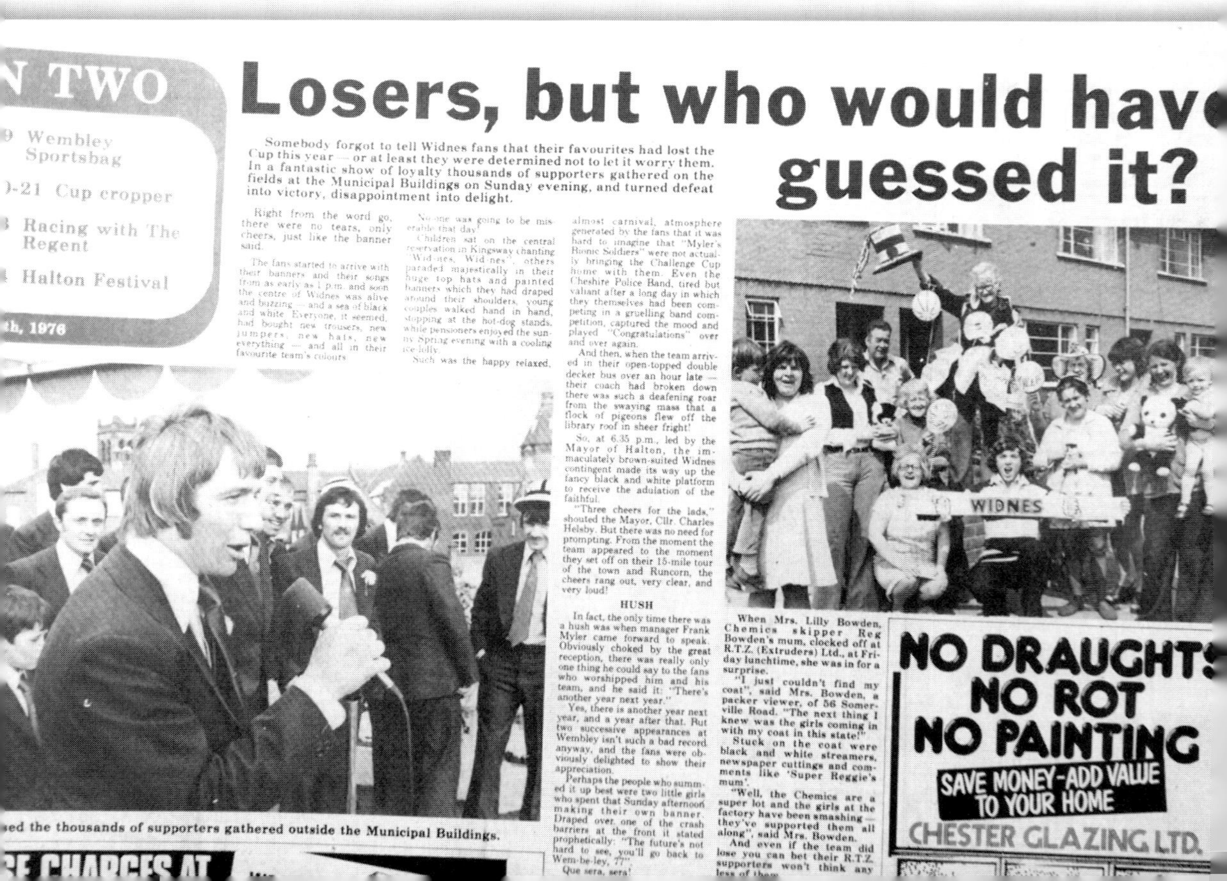

THE RUGBY LEAGUE CHALLENGE CUP COMPETITION

FINAL

SATURDAY, 7 MAY, 1977

LEEDS
VERSUS
WIDNES

WEMBLEY STADIUM

OFFICIAL PROGRAMME 25 PENCE

KICK OFF 3 p.m.

**1977 RUGBY LEAGUE CHALLENGE CUP FINAL
LEEDS V WIDNES**
Saturday 7 May 1977, Wembley Stadium, London

1977   *The Road to Wembley*

During the build up to the Final everyone was talking about it, the whole town was buzzing and everywhere was black and white. All this excitement was due to the Final of the Challenge Cup, but how did Widnes achieve their place at Wembley?

The fantastic road to Wembley began on the 13th February 1977. This was when Widnes played Bramley at McLaren Field and won 11-6.

The second round was at Naughton Park and Widnes beat Swinton 36-5, drawing Bradford Northern at home in the Quarter-Final. Widnes triumphed 19-5 to reach the last four stage of the Challenge Cup where they took on Hull Kingston Rovers, who they beat in the 1964 Final, at Headingley Stadium, Leeds. Once again Widnes had the upper hand on their East Coast rivals winning 14-5 in front of 17,000 fans.

Their opponents in the Final were the men from Headingley themselves, Leeds. They had begun their route to Wembley with an emphatic 40-6 win over Batley which they followed up with another home victory, this time defeating Barrow 21-11.

BACK ROW (*left to right*): Mal Aspey, Barry Sheridan, Ray Dutton, Jim Mills, John Wood, John Foran, Mick George, Alan Dearden, Eric Hughes.
FRONT ROW (*left to right*): Mick Adams, Peter Shaw, Steve Tilly, Keith Elwell, Reg Bowden (captain), Dave Eckersley, Nicky Kelly, Paul Woods, Dennis O'Neil.
Mascot: Paul Hamsbury

In the Quarter Final they travelled to Cumbria where they defeated Workington Town 8-2 which earned them a Semi-Final clash with St Helens at Central Park, Wigan, the Yorkshiremen running out winners 7-2 in front of just under 13,000 spectators.

The Game

On May 7th 1977, the Chemics were playing in the Challenge Cup Final at Wembley. That afternoon the Chemics were going head to head with Leeds. Widnes had a lot to make up on as they were defeated against St Helens the previous year at Wembley.

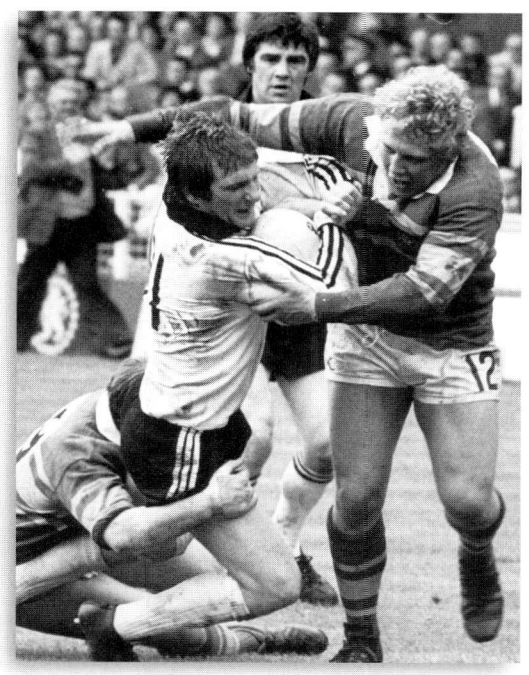

Above: Mick Adams is tacked by Leeds' second rower Phil Cockson as David Eckersley looks on

The Chemics had made a very impressive achievement as this was Widnes' third successful Wembley appearance; this had only ever been accomplished once before by Bradford. If the Chemics won this match it would have meant that Widnes' name would appeared for the fifth time on the trophy as winners.

On the afternoon of May 7th Widnes was more or less deserted, approximately 20,000 Chemics' fans had travelled south and paid £1.50 to watch the match. Those who hadn't gone were fixed to their television sets or radios keeping up with the tense drama. The adrenaline would have been superb.

On the day of the match all shops were closed and the streets empty, with this Widnes was a ghost town. At Wembley Stadium there were 80,871 fans hoping to see their team win, it was sure to be a memorable day, whether win or lose.

Widnes were leading at half time with 7-5 with a tremendous try from Mal Aspey who dodged three defenders in order to get a spectacular try between the posts, and two goals from Ray Dutton. However Leeds pulled back and Widnes unfortunately lost 16-7.

Ray French, who was a dual code rugby player before becoming a commentator for the BBC wrote about his 'top ten Challenge Cup Final shocks' Ray selected the Widnes versus Leeds match as eighth.

He stated; "Beaten in the 1976 Final by St Helens, Widnes were tipped to make amends in their third straight Final appearance. But they fell short again as Leeds, hit back from a 7-5 half-time deficit to triumph."

At the 1977 Challenge Cup Final John Foran was substitute forward. When we asked John why he was substitute, he answered; "Well, I was injured in the Quarter Final but I kept on playing, I didn't go off, but I was substituted in the last ten minutes because of my injury. Therefore I lost my place and unfortunately I was only a substitute for this Wembley."

Although John was only on the bench, the team was still good. By asking John what he thought of the 1977 team, we found out that; "Widnes were a much better team in 77, they were like Leeds are today. We were named the 'Cup Kings', because we seemed to win everything, and were the holders of the Lancashire Cup for the third successive year."

By interviewing John Foran we found out that Mick Adams had a superstition, John told us that Mick always had to go out of the tunnel last, because whenever he did, they always seemed to win. This was not true for the match against Leeds though. He also said that Ray Dutton always put his right sock and right boot on first. And that Jim Mills always went the toilet before the match.

Below: 'It's your Round...' Mick Adams demonstrates the true spirit of Rugby League by congratulating Graham Eccles of Leeds

At the 1977 Challenge Cup Final Jim Mills was the front row forward. When we asked Jim what the build up to the Final was like, he answered; "I can remember people from home telling me that during the game Widnes was like a ghost town. The Chemics were favourite to win the match, and as a result of this we went to Wembley expecting to win, and the fans were eager to see a win."

By interviewing Jim we found out what he thought led to the loss of the Final; "Even though we were winning at half time, I have always thought that everything went wrong in the first few minutes. This is because we were making silly errors, and after this there was nothing we could do. Therefore the match was lost to Leeds."

Ray Dutton, playing his third consecutive Final said the atmosphere was just as good at the Stadium. "What I probably remember the most from the game was having an argument with the referee when Leeds centre Les Dyl scored his try. I thought it was 'obstruction' and I certainly told the ref that!"

Paul Hansbury was also making his second Wembley appearance. "I was more confident this time, I knew the format but we still got beat!

RUGBY LEAGUE CHALLENGE CUP FINAL
Saturday 7 May 1977, Wembley Stadium, London

LEEDS	T	G	P	WIDNES	T	G	P
	3	4	16		1	2	7
B. Murrell				R. Dutton		2	
A. Smith				S. Wright			
N. Hague				M. Aspey	1		
L. Dyl	1			D. Eckersley			
J. Atkinson	1			D. O'Neill			
J. Holmes				E. Hughes			
K. Dick	1	4		R. Bowden Capt			
M. Harrison				W. Ramsey			
D. Ward				K. Elwell			
S. Pitchford				J. Mills			
G. Eccles				A. Dearden			
P. Cookson				M. Adams			
S. Fearnley				D. Laughton			
Subs				*Subs*			
D. Smith				M. George			
R. Dickinson				J. Foran			

Referee: J V Moss (Manchester)
Half Time: 5-7; Attendance: 80,871

The Homecoming

Four thousand fans turned up outside the Municipal Building and despite the team bus being two hours late the crowd was good-humoured and as the coach arrived the cheers rang out! As the team strolled from the coach to the special dias, waving to the crowd – it was Chemicsmania!

Coach Frank Myler was the first to speak to the crowd. "Thank you once again. I know we didn't win yesterday but we'll be trying twice as hard next year to bring the Cup back to you."

Captain Reg Bowden added "On behalf of the team I want to thank you all for your support throughout the season. Yesterday you outshone the Leeds fans in every aspect."

Winger Stuart Wright said "I think you're all fantastic" before, to the delight of the crowd, revealing that he was, after all, 'bionic'!

Jim and the team went to Wembley expecting to win, and the fans were waiting for a win. When we asked what the fans were like on their return, he replied;

"Despite the fact we had lost the fans were tremendous, and on our return the streets were packed with thousands of supporters, most of whom were wearing their Wembley colours. The fans were ready to give their players a hero's welcome home."

In his speech to the crowd Jim echoed the words of Frank Myler, "I can assure you we'll be trying twice as hard next year to get there again and bring the Cup back."

Following the speeches the players boarded an open-topped double decker bus to tour the town before ending up at Naughton Park.

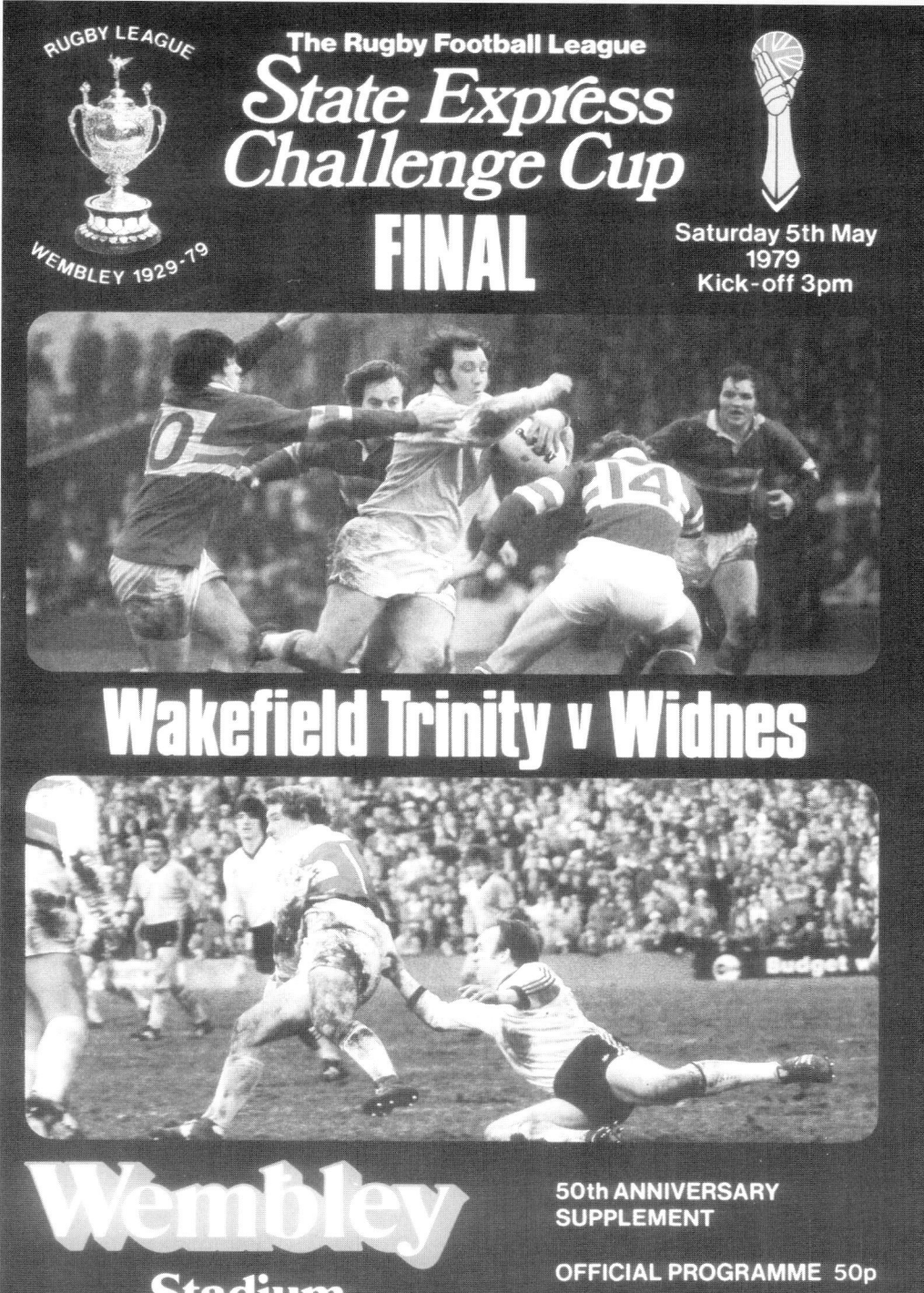

**1979 RUGBY LEAGUE CHALLENGE CUP FINAL
WAKEFIELD V WIDNES**
Saturday 5 May 1979, Wembley Stadium, London

1979 The Road to Wembley

Nineteen seventy nine saw the world of sponsorship come to Rugby League as the Challenge Cup became the State Express Challenge Cup and having been beaten in the Quarter-Final the previous year the Chemics were determined to return to their spiritual home of Wembley.

In the first round of the competition Widnes were drawn at home to Workington Town and despite a gutsy performance from the Cumbrians, the homeside were victors 12-5. Naughton Park was the venue for Widnes' second round tie and the Cherry and Whites of Wigan were accounted for 21-5.

In the Quarter Finals the Chemics crossed the Pennines for Huddersfield and comfortably defeated the Claret and Golds 14-0 which set up a Semi-Final clash with Bradford Northern.

The game took place at Station Road, Swinton and with just over 14,000 fans there, Widnes won by 14-11 to secure a place in the Final against Wakefield Trinity. The Yorkshire side had defeated neighbours Featherstone Rovers in the first round by 10-7 before beating Oldham 19-7 at The Watersheddings in the second round.

Their Quarter Final tie saw them entertain Barrow who they defeated 8-5 earning a Semi-Final match with St Helens at Headingley Stadium which they won 9-7.

Widnes 1978/79 with the Challenge Cup, John Player Trophy, BBC2 Floodlit Trophy and Lancashire Cup

The Game

The Final will not be remembered as a classic but perhaps for the fact that the man-of-the match trophy went to a player on the losing side, Wakefield Trinity stand-off David Topliss. In fact the first 40 minutes saw defences on top with the teams turning round with the scoreline 0-0.

Widnes took the lead nine minutes into the second half when winger Mick Burke landed a long-range penalty goal following a tackle by Bill Ashurst on Eric Hughes.

Below: Captain Reg Bowden leads out his team against Wakefield Trinity

Widnes extended their lead on the hour mark when right wing Stuart Wright made a 30 yard break and then kicked ahead, outpacing the covering defenders to score in the corner. Burke landed a superb touchline conversion and Widnes led 7-0. With just a quarter of the game to go an Elwell drop goal increased this lead. Wakefield replied with a try from their right wing, Andy Fletcher, but the game was made safe with 10 minutes on the clock as a drop goal from David Eckersley was followed by a fine individual try from Hughes who took the Wakefield defence on on the outside.

Perhaps the happiest member of the Widnes party was Paul Hansbury. "It was great to win at last, you could say it was third time lucky. I don't know what would have happened if we'd lost but at least I was no longer a jinx!"

Doug Laughton making yet another break against Wakefield Trinity

1979 RUGBY LEAGUE CHALLENGE CUP FINAL
Saturday 5 May 1979, Wembley Stadium, London

WAKEFIELD	T	G	P	WIDNES	T	G	P
	1	0	3		2	4	12
L. Sheard				D. Eckersley	1		
A. Fletcher	1			S. Wright	1		
K. Smith				M. Aspey			
S. Diamond				M. George			
B. Juliff				M. Burke		2	
D. Topliss				E. Hughes	1		
M. Lampkowski				R. Bowden Capt			
J. Burke				J. Mills			
A. McCurrie				K. Elwell	1		
T. Skerrett				G. Shaw			
Keith Rayne				M. Adams			
W. Ashurst				A. Dearden			
G. Idle				D. Laughton			
Subs				*Subs*			
T. Midgely				M. O'Neill			
Kevin Rayne				D. Hull			

Referee: J Jackson (Pudsey)
Half Time: 0-0; Attendance: 94,218

Below: Eric Hughes evades the covering tackle of Keith Rayne to score for the Chemics

The Homecoming

A heroes welcome awaited the Widnes side as they brought the Challenge Cup back home the next day. The streets were filled with black and white and despite cold, wet weather, a crowd of thousands gathered in front of the Municipal Building to welcome the team home.

The crowds began to gather on the field in front of the Municipal Building long before the scheduled arrival of 5.30pm and they were kept entertained by the Halton District Band.

As in previous years the team had travelled home by coach as far as Burtonwood Services where they swopped their coach for an open-topped double decker bus courtesy of the Merseyside Passenger Transport Executive.

Wives and girlfriends sat below while the victorious team and officials paraded the Challenge Cup round the streets of Widnes waving to cheering fans. Following their tour of the town the team arrived at the Municipal Building to an ecstatic reception from the crowd as the band struck up 'Congratulations'.

The Mayor and Mayoress officially welcomed the team back and Cllr Parr stated, "You have heard of the Magnificent Seven, well these are the Magnificent Thirteen."

The biggest cheer of the occasion came when captain Reg Bowden held the Cup aloft. "The support at Wembley was terrific, wherever we looked there was black and white."

One by one the players were called to the microphone and the Cup was filled with champagne before being passed around some of the fans.

Players were given presents with Jim Mills loaded with hats, teddy bears and an umbrella which was just as well as the rain poured down.

The team returned to the bus and gave a rousing chorus of 'Singing in the Rain' before continuing for a further tour of the town and returning to Naughton Park where their own celebrations were to take place.

WIDNES FOOTBALL CLUB

CELEBRATION DINNER

TO CELEBRATE THE WINNING OF THE RUGBY LEAGUE STATE EXPRESS CHALLENGE CUP

WIDNES 12 pts   WAKEFIELD TRINITY 3 pts

EURO CREST HOTEL, MAIDENHEAD
SATURDAY, 5th MAY, 1979

Big Jim Mills in reflective mood after yet another Wembley success

Over the P.A. system, club chairman, Tom Smith, won the fans' immediate ... was a great reception at Wembley ... like to thank you all ... it was superb.

HANDS reach out for the Cup, held firmly by Keith Elwell.

FOR THE HEROES

ASSISTANT coach Harry Dawson yodelled his 'Black ... Sunday evening. ... familiar to Widnesians — wind and rain to welcome Widnes home 40 minutes ... 'White Magic' went ... again. ... "Give them a big welcome, patient with us all season. aren't they great!" ... classical open top It's been marvellous, double decker bus

Three Fives Challenge

The Rugby Football League

Three Fives Challenge Cup

1981 Final

Hull K.R. v Widnes

Saturday 2nd May Kick-off 3pm

Wembley Stadium

OFFICIAL PROGRAMME 60p

1981 RUGBY LEAGUE CHALLENGE CUP FINAL
HULL KR V WIDNES
Saturday 2 May 1981, Wembley Stadium, London

1981 The Road to Wembley

As the Challenge Cup drew closer all eyes were on the draw for the first round and Widnes fans were delighted to be paired with Doncaster at Naughton Park. So it seemed were the players as they scored 50 points without reply.

The Chemics were drawn at home in the second round but this game was a much closer affair as they overcame Yorkshire opposition again, this time Castleford, but by only two points, 7-5.

In the Quarter Finals Widnes travelled to Post Office Road, home to Featherstone Rovers who they had beaten in the 1976 Semi Final, and this time won comfortably 21-5.

Once again fate threw Widnes together with rivals Warrington, this time at the Semi-Final stage, where in front of 12,500 fans at Central Park, Wigan the Chemics won 17-9.

Hull KR were to be Widnes' opponents in the Final, a repeat of the 1964 Final. They had started their road to Wembley with an 18-13 home win over Barrow and followed this up with a second home win, this time defeating York 23-7.

The Robins were drawn at home again in the Quarter Finals and accounted for Salford 19-8 to set up a clash with St Helens at Headingley. Hull KR ran out comfortable winners in front of over 17,000 fans to set up the replay of the 1964 match.

Below: The 'Cup Kings' celebrate... left to right: Les Gorley, Andy Gregory, Mike O'Neill, Keith Bentley, John Myler and Eric Hughes

The Game

Above: Mick George on his way to the try-line and (below) touches down

Unlike 1964, Widnes went into the games as favourites and the performance of the team on the day lived up to this pre-match billing as they dominated the game.

It took under five minutes for the Chemics to take the lead as Mick Burke, joining the line from his full-back position, chipped ahead and regathered the ball to touchdown.

Above: The Widnes bench look on intently...

Right: Full back Mick Burke adds another two points

Rovers' wing Steve Hubbard pulled two points back with a penalty goal but Burke replied in kind to re-establish Widnes' lead, a lead which was extended when Mick George touched down and Burke's conversion made it 10-2.

Hubbard added a second penalty but a drop goal from Mick Adams saw Widnes go into the break with a seven point advantage. It took Widnes just two minutes to surge ahead in the second half with Andy Gregory jinking through the Robins defence to touchdown. Burke's conversion plus a penalty stretched the lead and even though Chris Burton grabbed a consolation try from Hull KR, Hubbard adding his third goal, it wasn't enough.

Left: "We've won the Cup..." An overjoyed Widnes bench celebrate their victory

1981 RUGBY LEAGUE CHALLENGE CUP FINAL
Saturday 2 May 1981, Wembley Stadium, London

HULL KR	T	G	P	WIDNES	T	G	P
	1	3	9		3	5	18
D. Hall				M. Burke	1	4	
S. Hubbard		3		S. Wright			
M. Smith				M. George	1		
P. Hogan				E. Cunningham			
P. Muscroft				K. Bentley			
S. Hartley				E. Hughes			
P. Harkin				A. Gregory	1		
R. Holdstock				M. O'Neill			
D. Watkinson				K. Elwell			
S. Crooks				B. Lockwood			
P. Lowe				L. Gorley			
C. Burton	1			E. Prescott			
L. Casey				M. Adams Capt		1	
Subs				*Subs*			
P. Proctor				J. Myler			
J. Millington				G. Shaw			

Referee: G Kershaw (Easingwold)
Half Time: 4-11; Attendance: 92,496

Right: Brian Lockwood congratulates Mick Burke at the end of the 1981 Challenge Cup Final

Below: 'Cup Kings' - Widnes celebrate yet again in 1981

The Homecoming

The Municipal Building was once again the venue for the Chemics' homecoming from Wembley Stadium.

The partying was led by assistant coach Harry Dawson who yodelled his "Black Magic" party-piece for the benefit of the thousands of people who had turned up to greet their heroes.

'Black and White Magic' might have been more appropriate as they were the only colours on display on Sunday afternoon.

The players and officials were welcomed onto the specially built platform by the Mayor, Councillor Kath Gerard who implored the crowd to 'give them a cheer, aren't they great!'

Captain Mick Adams spoke to the crowd first. "Thank you for being very patient with us all season. It's been marvellous, marvellous."

After about twenty minutes the players climbed aboard a classic open top bus for a tour of the town and it seemed as if the whole population had come out to cheer.

WIDNES FOOTBALL CLUB
END-OF-SEASON DINNER

CHALLENGE CUP WINNERS 1981

WIDNES FOOTBALL SOCIAL CLUB
FRIDAY, MAY 22nd, 1981

THE STATE EXPRESS RUGBY LEAGUE CHALLENGE CUP FINAL 1979

WIDNES 12 • WAKEFIELD TRINITY 3

"The Cup Kings"

R Bowden — Captain
D. Laughton — Player Coach

M. Adams	D. Eckersley	J. Mills
M. Aspey	K. Elwell	M. O'Neill
M. Burke	M. George	G. Shaw
A. Dearden	E. Hughes	S. Wright
	D. Hull	

Club President — J. Davies
Chairman — J. Woodward
Secretary / General Manager — H. Greenwood

Committee Members:

H. Ditchfield	R.H. Faulkner	J. Hayes
D. K. Morgan	F. Nyland	R. Owen
J. Preston		T. Smith

Physiotherapist — F. Tobin
Assistant Coaches — H. Dawson & J. Mills
Hon. Surgeon — Dr. G. Tandy
Consultant Surgeon — A. G. O'Malley

WEEKLY NEWS, WEEK ENDING MAY 8th, 1981
WIDNES AT WEMBLEY 1981

...LY AFFAIR... Wembley hero Andy Gregory shares the Cup glory with his biggest fan, grandad Harold

---

WIDNES WEEKLY NEWS
FRIDAY MAY 8 1981 — POLITICALLY INDEPENDENT — 105th YEAR — PRICE 12p

IT'S OURS!

"You have my personal guarantee that we will never be beaten on any G-Plan price. And that's a fact."
— Andrew D. Harris

**1982 RUGBY LEAGUE CHALLENGE CUP FINAL
HULL V WIDNES**
Saturday 1 May 1982, Wembley Stadium, London

1982 The Road to Wembley

Twenty three years ago and Madness with the song 'House of Fun was top of the charts with Widnes on their way to Wembley too. Widnes had previously been to Wembley 10 times, winning the Challenge Cup 6 times, the John Player cup twice, the Lancashire Cup 5 times, the Premiership Trophy and BBC2's Floodlit Trophy.

1982 also had other memorable events such as the State Express Challenge Cup campaign which was valued at £100,000 which was the first ever 6 figure sponsorship sum commanded by the 13-a-side code.

The first round tie was against Cardiff away, this was a long coach ride from Widnes into the South of Wales for the Widnes players and coaching staff.

10 minutes into the game Tony Myler opened up the scoring and then his brother John added the extra 2 points, 12 minutes later Tony Myler crossed the try line again with a 30 yard scamper through the Cardiff defence plus John added the extras. When the half time whistle was blown the score was Widnes 12-5 Cardiff.

Widnes were playing well and Tony and John Myler were playing out of their skins, John Myler's goal kicking was world class. In the second half, the first 15 minutes was a defensive battle but then finally Widnes came through when John Basnett capitalised on a stray pass by the Cardiff centre, he intercepted that stray pass and ran 75 yards untouched and scored a fantastic try in dreadful conditions.

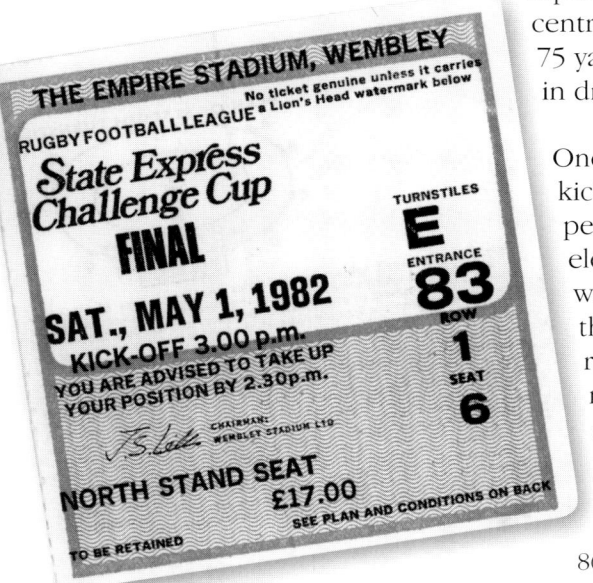

Once again John Myler converted the goal kick and then 5 minutes later Widnes won a penalty from 40 yards out and Myler elected to goal kick and struck the ball with great velocity and it sailed through the goal posts over the black dot. The end result was 19-8 to Widnes, the man of the match was John Myler and the attendance was 5,452 with 1,205 of the attendance Widnes fans.

The second round tie against Wigan away was a very tricky encounter but spirits were high in the Widnes first team, this was a local derby and a few of the Widnes players were former Wigan players or were born and raised in Wigan.

In the first half it took 25 minutes for Widnes to score and the try came from Eddie Cunnigham with a pile driving 10 yard burst into Wigan's defensive line, John Myler converted the try. Half time arrived and the score was Wigan 7-5 Widnes, the Widnes outfit were very tired in this defensive battle and were very sloppy when they were attacking, they conceded a few penalties which cost them dearly.

Above: Keiron O'Loughlin looks to offload in the 1982 Challenge Cup Final

In the second half it was another ferocious defensive battle, 21 minutes in and Widnes were given a penalty and John Myler stepped up to take the goal kick under immense pressure and he came through with a spectacular goal kick which brought the game level at 7-7.

The game was an end to end affair throughout but 3 minutes from the end Wigan slipped up and gave Widnes a penalty and John Myler stepped up very confidently and struck the ball through the goal posts and sent Widnes through to the Quarter Final.

The game finished at 9-7 in Widnes' favour, the man of the match was Eddie Cunningham and the attendance was 17,467 with 4,073 of the crowd Widnes fans.

The Quarter Final was a tough encounter against Bradford away and this was a battle of the roses affair, Lancashire versus Yorkshire. In the early stages it was all Widnes who went 6-0 up thanks to a typical opportunist try by John Basnett, who dribbled the ball 60 yards before touching down just inside the dead-ball line. John Myler's conversion and a rare drop goal from Eric Prescott were the other points scored at that stage.

But the home team were not going to give up without a fight and they gradually turned the deficit into an 8-6 lead. David Redfearn got their try and Dean Carroll added a conversion, a penalty and a drop goal.

With only seconds to go it looked as if the Widnes Wembley dream was over for another year but Tony Myler tried one last desperate kick ahead and, despite protests from the Bradford players, referee Stan Wall decided he was obstructed. Tony's brother John kept his cool to convert the penalty to make the final score 8-8. Man of the match was John Basnett and the attendance was 9,583 and 2,769 of the crowd were Widnes fans.

This resulted in a replay which was at Naughton Park, this was the first and last time Widnes had a home advantage in the 1982 competition. In the first half Widnes were 6-0 down 25 minutes into the game but 30 minutes into the game prop Les Gorley pile-drived through the defence and John Myler converted the try which left Widnes 6-5 down at half time.

The second half was very intense with a Semi Final place at stake and 5 minutes from time Andy Gregory came up trumps with a spectacular try where he backed up John Myler's 30 yard scamper, Myler offloading the ball to Gregory and the scrum half crossed the whitewash for the try. Then John Myler converted the try with a kick from 25 yards infront of the posts which won the game for Widnes and booked their place in the Semi Finals. Man of the Match was Andy Gregory and the attendance was 11,877.

In the Semi Finals it was Widnes' hardest game against the fierce team Leeds, who had an outstanding defensive record and were a very fast attacking outfit.

Below: A unique photograph of ex-Widnes players in a Testimonial Match. Scrum half Jimmy Boylan takes on hooker Derek Hammond as left to right, Bob Blackwood, Vince Karalius, Ray French, Jack Hayes and Abbie Lamb look on

This Semi Final was held at Swinton. Once again the Chemics had to come from behind - not once but twice. Leeds were first on the scoreboard with a try by David Heron, Kevin Dick's conversion giving them a 5-0 lead.

Widnes were struggling to make any impact on the

game but suddenly they hit form in the second half and John Basnett scored two almost identical tries near the left corner, both followed some great passing, and his side now led 6-5.

But Leeds bounced back, Les Dyl scored a late try and Widnes were in trouble, 8-6 down. Maybe remembering the last round, Mick Adams kicked ahead in the dying seconds and seemed to be looking for a penalty for obstruction. The referee didn't agree this time but amazingly the ball hit the crossbar and bounced into the arms of Keiron O'Loughlin who couldn't believe his luck as he scored under the posts. John Myler's conversion was the last action of the game, making the final score 11-8 and Widnes were into the Final at Wembley for the second year running, and were willing to defend their title.

Soon after the game the Widnes players found out that they were about to face Hull in the Final and they knew they were going to have a fierce and hard match against them. Man of the match was John Basnett and the attendance was 12,974 with half of them Widnes fans.

Widnes had doubts about two key players going into the game. Centre Eddie Cunningham had suffered a neck injury and coach Doug Laughton had publically commented that he wouldn't play anyone who wasn't 100% fit.

Meanwhile Eric Hughes had a date with the disciplinary committee on the Thursday before the Final. Widnes decided to hire a helicopter to fly Eric from their Wembley base to Leeds and the gamble paid off as Hughes escaped suspension.

The Game

The road to Wembley was a tough one for Widnes and it was all going to pay off for them at the Final or so they thought. Widnes town was buzzing the week before the Final.

However one man probably more nervous than the players at Wembley that day was the BBC's Ray French.

"It was my first Wembley Final, following in the footsteps of the great Eddie Waring. I'd done all my research on the players and was in my commentary position three hours before kick-off.

"A bit early some might say but the lift to the commentary box was known to be temperamental and I had visions of being stuck in it and not being able to get out before the game started!

"I also had to watch what I ate as at a previous television game at Headingley I'd got a fish bone stuck in my throat. It took forever for the medical staff to get it out and at one stage it looked like I wouldn't be able to commentate!

"As if commentating on my first Wembley Final wasn't nerve-wracking enough it was the time when the Falklands conflict was on and the British forces were due to land at Goose Green.

"I'd been told by my producer that as soon as the landing had started I had to hand immediately to the BBC newsroom where an update would be given.

"So as the game got underway I knew my commentary could turn out something like, 'It's Widnes on the attack, O'Neill to Gregory, Gregory to Cunningham who's going for the line… and now over to Moira Stewart in the BBC Newsroom for a Newsflash!'

Right: Keiron O'Loughlin looks for support in the 1982 Challenge Cup Final

"As it happens the landing took place early in the first half and I was able to get on with commentating on the game."

The ground's atmosphere was deafening right before kick off with the pre-match community singing focusing on patriotic songs given the world events at that time. On the pitch there was a battle going on with both teams looking for the upperhand but at the end of forty minutes the scores were tied 6-6. Keith Elwell had opened the scoring for Widnes with a drop goal and a try from Eddie Cunningham goaled by Mick Burke gave Widnes their six points whilst Hull's Sammy Lloyd landed three penalty goals, all for offences by Eric Hughes!

The second half saw Widnes take the lead as a Cunningham try goaled by Andy Gregory followed by a length of the field interception try from Stuart Wright put the Chemics in a commanding position at 14-6 with fifteen minutes to play.

Hull hadn't given the game up and tries from Steve Norton and Dane O'Hara, plus one Sammy Lloyd goal levelled the scores to force a replay which was going to be held at Leeds United AFC.

1982 RUGBY LEAGUE CHALLENGE CUP FINAL
Saturday 1 May 1982, Wembley Stadium, London

HULL	T	G	P	WIDNES	T	G	P
	2	4	14		3	3	14
G. Kemble				M. Burke		1	
D. O'Hara	1			S. Wright	1		
T. Day				K. O'Loughlin			
S. Evans				E. Cunningham	2		
P. Prendiville				J. Basnett			
D. Topliss				E. Hughes			
K. Harkin				A. Gregory		1	
T. Skerrett				M. O'Neill			
R. Wileman				K. Elwell			1
C. Stone				B. Lockwood			
M. Crane				L. Gorley			
S. Lloyd		4		E. Prescott			
S. Norton	1			M. Adams Capt			
Subs				*Subs*			
J. Leuluai				A. Myler			
L. Crooks				S. O'Neill			

Referee: F Lindop (Wakefield)
Half Time: 6-6; Attendance: 92,147

The Replay

The replay was a very much anticipated contest. Widnes had played six games prior to this Final replay game and the side looked very worn out and tired before the game

It was a very cold evening and the players went through two tubs of Vaseline to keep them warm. In the first half Hull dominated Widnes and had most of the possession with a Mick Burke penalty the Chemics only response to tries from Kemble and Topliss plus a Lee Crooks goal.

In the second half the Widnes team showed a bit of spirit when Stuart Wright had crossed the white wash and Mick Burke converted the try with a beautifully struck goal kick which made the game 8-7 to Hull but 5 minutes after Hull scored a try and converted it to increase their lead and although Burke added a third goal a Crooks try, which he goaled himself, made the final score 18-9 in favour of Hull. Man of the match was Hull's captain David Topliss.

Even though Widnes did not retain the Challenge Cup it was not a bad year for the club. They had a good enough side to win more Challenge Cups in the future as you will find out!

Right: Hull's Paul Prendiville escapes the Widnes defence

The Rugby League
STATE EXPRESS CHALLENGE CUP

STATE EXPRESS CLASSIC EVENT

1982 Final Replay

Hull v Widnes

Leeds United AFC, 19th May 7.30 p.m.

Official Big Match Programme

50P

1982 RUGBY LEAGUE CHALLENGE CUP FINAL REPLAY
HULL V WIDNES
Wednesday 19 May 1982, Elland Road, Leeds

1982 RUGBY LEAGUE CHALLENGE CUP FINAL REPLAY
Wednesday 19 May 1982, Elland Road, Leeds

HULL	T	G	P	WIDNES	T	G	P
HULL	**4**	**3**	**18**	**WIDNES**	**1**	**3**	**9**
G. Kemble	1			M. Burke		3	
C. Sullivan				S. Wright	1		
J. Leulaui				K. O'Loughlin			
S. Evans				E. Cunningham			
P. Prendiville				J. Basnett			
D. Topliss	2			E. Hughes			
A. Dean				A. Gregory			
K. Tindall				M. O'Neill			
A. Duke				K. Elwell			
C. Stone				B. Lockwood			
T. Skerrett				L. Gorley			
L. Crooks	1	3		E. Prescott			
S. Norton				M. Adams Capt			
Subs				*Subs*			
T. Day				T. Myler			
M. Crane				F. Whitfield			

Referee: F Lindop (Wakefield)
Half Time: 8- 2; Attendance: 41,171

The Homecoming

Immediately after the first game both teams embarked on a dual lap of honour around the Stadium before returning to the dressing rooms. The Widnes players sat there in disbelief as they replayed in their minds the events of the last eighty minutes.

Man of the Match Eddie Cunningham looked to shoulder the blame for the Chemics despite scoring two tries.
"If I'd have been fully fit they wouldn't have scored their two tries," he said. Doug Laughton added that it was a real anti-climax and that in future the game should be decided on the day.

Despite this setback the players received a rapturous reception from the fans at Naughton Park on their return on Sunday evening. Speeches were made to the crowd but there was a sense of disappointment at the lack of the trophy but anticipation of the replay.

The Rugby League
STATE EXPRESS CHALLENGE CUP

STATE EXPRESS CLASSIC EVENT

WIDNES v. WIGAN

Wembley Stadium

1984 Final
5th May 3.00 p.m.

Official Programme 80p

1984 RUGBY LEAGUE CHALLENGE CUP FINAL
WIGAN V WIDNES
Saturday 5 May 1984, Wembley Stadium, London

1984 The Road to Wembley

The 1984 campaign got underway with Widnes having to take part in a Preliminary Round of the Challenge Cup with the Chemics drawn away to Carlisle in a game they won 20-12.

The draw for the first round was kind to Widnes and they entertained Dewsbury at Naughton Park winning at a canter by 54-10, running in 11 tries in the process.

Having defeated a 'new' team in the Preliminary Round the Chemics were on their travels again to take on another of the League's new boys in Fulham, a team which had been established three years earlier and included a nucleus of former Widnes players.

The game took place at Craven Cottage, the ground the rugby league side shared with their footballing counterparts and Widnes edged home 12-10 to earn a place in the Quarter Finals.

The Quarter Final saw Widnes return to Naughton Park and a home-tie with Hull Kingston Rovers which the Chemics won 21-10.

Widnes RLFC 1984

Once again the venue for the Semi-Finals was Station Road, Swinton and a Joe Lydon 'special' helped Widnes to a 15-4 victory and a return to the Twin Towers where they were to meet Wigan coached by their great adversary Alex Murphy.

Wigan's path to the Final began in Yorkshire where they were held 10-10 by Bramley before accounting for them 34-4 in the replay at Central Park.

In the second round they had another comfortable home victory, this time defeating fellow Lancastrians Oldham 30-6, which led to another derby in the Quarter-Final as they beat St Helens 16-7 at Knowsley Road.

Their opponents in the Semi-Final were York and in front of over 17,000 fans at Elland Road they progressed to the Final with a 14-8 victory.

The Game

In the 1984 Challenge Cup Final there were a few old rivalries ignited again as the Widnes side contained both former Wigan players and players who were born in Wigan.

On the morning of the game Joe Lydon wanted to go to Church so coach Vince Karalius arranged for him to go with legendary physiotherapist Frank Tobin.

Said Frank, "Vincent knew I was a practising Catholic and asked me to take Joe. Unfortunately by the time we got there Mass had finished but we still managed to light some candles."

For Steve O'Neill it was an extra special occasion as not only was he representing his home town club at Wembley but his brother Mike was also in the side.

In the build up to the Final the team spent some time training in Southport at a school where the rugby pitch was of a similar quality to that of Wembley. "The grass was like Wembley's to train on as it was heavy to play on and tired you out, so we tried to get used to playing on that sort of surface." said Steve.

Right: Wigan coach Alex Murphy receives some advice from two young Widnes fans

When they did get to Wembley for the game all of the team were very focused on what they had to do as they had come this far before but had not won. The dressing room saw various players follow their superstitious pre-match ritual and Steve was no exception as he always wanted to be the last player out of the dressing room.

Inside the Stadium the crowd was roaring for their team but the players were calm as the coach, Vince Karalius, had trained them not to get carried away with the atmosphere. It was quite intimidating for the players but they followed their coach's orders. There was a lot of pressure on the players as the club had the reputation of being the 'Cup Kings' and the fans, who had grown accustomed to the team winning trophies, were expecting a lot from the players.

The Widnes performance was highlighted by two sensational tries from Joe Lydon, a youngster plucked from under the noses of the Wigan club and who in 1975 had played against Widnes in the schoolboy curtain-raiser at Wembley.

Ironically the first points of the game came from Wigan centre Colin Whitfield, himself a Widnesian and future coach of the team.

Widnes' first points came through a Keiron O'Loughlin try, converted by Mick Burke and they increased their lead when

Les Gorley and Kevin Tamati combined to give Lydon the opportunity to race clear from inside his own half for a try which Burke goaled.

A 12-2 interval lead soon became 13-2 as Steve O'Neill landed a drop goal and the game was made safe 9 minutes from time when Lydon picked up a loose pass inside his own '25' and sped away, rounding debutant full-back Shaun Edwards to score one of the best tries ever seen at Wembley.

Wigan responded with an unconverted try from Kerry Hemsley but once again the Challenge Cup was Widnes-bound.

"As soon as the game finished Joe ran straight over and hugged me" added Tobin "It was a great moment."

In the dressing room after the game there were scenes of great joy. Steve O'Neill had found a friend in the crowd and brought him into the dressing room whilst Joe Lydon sat there for half-an-hour reflecting on what had happened.

Below: Eric Hughes (left) and Kevin Tamati lift the Challenge Cup

1984 RUGBY LEAGUE CHALLENGE CUP FINAL
Saturday 5 May 1984, Wembley Stadium, London

	T	G	P		T	G	P
WIGAN	1	1	6	**WIDNES**	3	4	19
S. Edwards				M. Burke		3	
D. Ramsdale				S. Wright			
D. Stephenson				E. Hughes			
C. Whitfield	1			J. Lydon		2	
H. Gill				J. Basnett			
M. Cannon				K. O'Loughlin	1		
G. Stephens				A. Gregory			
K. Hemsley		1		S. O'Neill	1		
H. Tamati				K. Elwell			
B. Case				K. Tamati			
G. West				L. Gorley			
M. Scott				M. O'Neill			
J. Pendlebury				M. Adams Capt			
Subs				*Subs*			
W. Elvin				D. Hulme			
B. Juliff				F. Whitfield			

Referee: W Thompson (Huddersfield)
Half Time: 2-12; Attendance: 80,116

For Paul Hansbury it was his first Final as an employee of Widnes. "When I left school I was lucky enough to get a job at Widnes and less than 12 months later I was back at Wembley. It was a bit nerve-wracking but as I was older I was able to take more in and enjoy it more, especially Joe's two tries."

Left: 'Checkmate...' Winger John Basnett celebrates success in 1984

The Homecoming

After the festivities of Cup Final night coach Vince Karalius had substitute David Hulme up early the next morning to go to Church prior to the coach journey back North.

As the coach reached the Burtonwood Services on the M62 the players transferred to an open-top bus for the remainder of the journey back to Widnes.

The bus made its way through the town and even though it was May it was very cold on top of the bus but it didn't stop the fans from lining the streets as the bus made its way to the homecoming.

STEVE O'Neill leads the chanting as Widnes commence their lap of honour

**1993 RUGBY LEAGUE CHALLENGE CUP FINAL
WIGAN V WIDNES**
Saturday 1 May 1993, Wembley Stadium, London

1993 *The Road to Wembley*

Widnes began their mission to Wembley in 1993, with a preliminary home fixture against Swinton on a cold night in January, along with the knowledge that the season hadn't gone off with a bang.

However, against all the odds, Paul Hulme led his team out to victory with an amazing 62-14 win. Although Widnes triumphed so comfortably in the preliminaries, thoughts of even reaching the Final had to be put on hold; four gruelling Challenge Cup matches stood in their way. Or so they thought...

Two matches were what fans would call "walk-overs". With a disadvantage of three away ties in succession, Widnes travelled up to Whitehaven for the first. After yet another cold afternoon, an impressive 20-8 win gave Widnes the satisfaction and the result that they both wanted and deserved.

Sheffield Eagles 6, Widnes 52. Who thought that this would have been the score line after the final hooter? After a tough game, a tremendous performance from a fantastically skilled Widnes pack in the second round, took them through to the

Below: Widnes celebrate their Semi-Final victory over Leeds

Left: Jonathan Davies out-strips James Lowes of Leeds in the Challenge Cup Semi-Final at Central Park, Wigan

Quarter-Finals. In the past, several teams had reached a Wembley Final with no set-backs. So, when it came to Widnes' turn, the team and coaching staff thought the same. The self-belief was sky high and the lads were up for it, but unfortunately they couldn't deliver what certain teams had done before them.

Both Widnes and Hull KR were unaware of what was to be in store for them. They were also unaware of the fact that they were going to be a part of a memorable and one truly unforgettable Quarter-Final. After getting off to some positive starts in the previous rounds, Hull KR almost stopped Widnes dead in their tracks, letting them touch down over the line with only one unconverted try. At the end of the 80 minutes and the score being 4-4, there was just one solution for the problem that arose; a replay.

Jonathan Davies shared his recollections with us. "With all the hype of the replay, we weren't going to let this second chance slip. It was about 9 degrees but the freezing cold weather didn't put the boys off, even though I couldn't feel my legs!" Eventually, the confidence of the Widnes side was at its peak. But for someone, his confidence got the better of him.

Above: Widnes RLFC 1992-93

"With all the goings on in the game, I should have been sent off the pitch," Jonathan announced. "I was left unconscious after being elbowed in the chops! I didn't like it but I think it was entertaining for the spectators to watch." After some overwhelming spurts of confidence, Widnes came out the better team with a score of 16-11 and more importantly, a place in the Semi-Finals.

Lady luck was never really with Widnes when it came to Semi-Final fixtures. If they were determined to go any further, they would have had to break the curse of being on the wrong side of three previous Semi-Final results, two of them being against St. Helens. Drawing a tie against Leeds wasn't what Widnes were hoping for.

Paul Hulme revealed his nervousness to us. "It was ominous Leeds were favourites going into that match. There was obviously an air of nervousness. It was fourth time lucky really, we were placed in a semi and we knew that to get to Wembley we just had to take it to Leeds and beat them."

The match seemed to be a little personal for the Widnes lads. They were up against an international and well known ex teammate, Alan Tait, and also, their former coach, Doug Laughton. With a convincing 39-4 win over Leeds, it was a shock to everyone, but Widnes made it perfectly clear that they were happy with the result. "We had no words of comfort for them," Paul revealed. "We enjoyed every minute of it."

Well, they did it. Widnes survived the rounds and achieved what they longed for; a place at the Challenge Cup Final. It was just a matter of being the last team standing at the end of it.

The opponents in the Final where to be Wigan, thus setting up a repeat of the 1984 'Joe Lydon' Final. Wigan had won the previous five Finals but this did not stop them also being drawn out of the hat for the preliminary round and had comfortably beaten Hull 40-2.

In the first round they travelled to Dewsbury and came away with a 20-4 victory which earned them a home tie with St Helens in the second round, a game they won easily by 23-3.

In the Quarter-Final they were again on their travels over the Pennines and just edged out Halifax 19-18 to line up a Semi-Final encounter with Bradford Northern at Elland Road, Leeds.

A crowd of over 20,000 was in the stadium to see the Lancastrians triumph 15-6 and set up an all-Lancashire Challenge Cup Final.

The people of Widnes were very excited to hear, that following the defeat of Leeds in the Semi Finals, their team was next to meet the in-form side of the day, Wigan, in the Final at Wembley Stadium on May 1st 1993.

There had been fears that having lost top class try scorer and player in Martin Offiah, the chances of winning through to the Final were slim. However, who would have thought that the opponents for the mighty Wigan All-Stars, consisting of Martin Offiah, amongst others, would have been his old club, Widnes.

As you could imagine, the atmosphere in the town was reaching fever pitch. It had been 4 years since Widnes had beaten Canberra Raiders in the World Club championship and even longer since their last appearance at the "twin towers".

Homes were decorated, shops and offices displayed banners wishing the team luck for the big day, some hoisted black and white flags, others filled windows with black and white scarves and pictures of the Challenge Cup trophy.

The main street and shopping areas of the town were amassed with 'black and white'.

People who remembered the cup run of the 70's and 80's were already beginning to organise themselves into groups and parties. Coaches were being hired, hotels were getting booked, and some parties were even booking trains their numbers were so many. All the good, old, Widnes organisational skills were being put to good use once again.

As the day of the Final approached more and more people could be seen walking round the town with Widnes shirts and hats.

The whole town was buzzing once again in anticipation of the Final at Wembley, which was considered by some of the older townsfolk to be their "second home".

The Game

Every year in the rugby league calendar, the Challenge Cup Final is arguably the most awaited eighty minutes of the entire season. Just being a part of it breeds excitement and a sense of pride. Fans do everything they can, in the week leading up to the Final, to support and encourage their team. However, thirteen tense faces sat in the changing room an hour before the kick off of what should be a rugby player's most exciting eighty minutes that season. When it was Wigan's turn to take on the Chemics, it was no exception.

Everyone in the Widnes camp had superstitions and strange habits for the Final. Such as putting socks or boots on the left foot first. Some players even had underwear that they wore for every game, just to see if they were lucky. They believed that if these habits had worked for the games before the Final, then they would work for the match that mattered the most.

The mood was on a high when the players stepped off the coach, but when they were stood in the tunnel, it was a different story. Paul Hulme spoke of his experience. "When you're waiting in the tunnel it suddenly dawns on you. If you want to be nervous, then that's the time to be." As soon as one foot was stepped on the grass, it was overwhelming. Both Widnes and Wigan were up for it and the atmosphere was

Above: Richie Eyres scores Widnes' opening try at Wembley in 1993

phenomenal. All the crowd was waiting for now, was the boot to kick off the game.

The Widnes team were seen as the underdogs on the day but they immediately gave the Wiganers a run for their money. In the seventh minute, the first try was scored. Bobby Goulding created a gap for the impressive Richie Eyres to touch down. The try was converted by the mighty boot of Jonathan Davies, 6-0 to Widnes. However, it didn't take the Wigan Cup Kings long to reply and within just a few short minutes they levelled the score with a try by Kelvin Skerrett, converted by Frano Botica.

Still in the first half of the game and the next try came along by the soon to retire, 37 year old Kurt Sorensen. Again the try was converted by Jonathan Davies, re-establishing Widnes' six-point advantage. Was it deja-vu? Widnes' John Devereux caught a Wigan kick and ran towards Martin 'Chariots' Offiah and subsequently spilled the ball. The quickest to react was Offiah; scooping up the loose ball, he passed to Dean Bell who ran unopposed for a very simple touch down. Bell's try was converted by the record breaking Botica, who had now scored 176 goals in a season, taking the record away from Fred Griffiths which he set in 1959. Just before half time, the brilliant boot of Botica once again caused problems for the Chemics by scoring a penalty goal. The half time score was 14-12 for Wigan.

Second half and it wasn't long before Wigan extended their lead. Sam Panapa scored a four pointer from a pass by Dean Bell. Could the boot of Botica drive the nail any further into the coffin for the black and whites? Of course it could. The score was now 20-14 in the Riversiders favour. Could it get any worse?

The 65th minute of the match and Widnes were now destined to fail. Richie Eyres was sent off for an elbow to the head of his ex teammate, Martin Offiah.

Below: A dejected Widnes captain Paul Hulme leads David Myers and Harvey Howard down the famous Wembley steps

Now into the final minutes of the game and an ugly brawl erupted when Bobby Goulding tackled Jason Robinson with a late and high tackle. Widnes had finally put the lid on the coffin and their hopes of another Wembley victory had disappeared into thin air. This match was the last match that Widnes would ever play at the magnificent twin towered, Wembley Stadium.

1993 RUGBY LEAGUE CHALLENGE CUP FINAL
Saturday 1 May 1993, Wembley Stadium, London

WIGAN	T	G	P	WIDNES	T	G	P
	3	4	20		2	3	14
S. Hampson				S. Spruce			
J. Robinson				J. Devereux			
J. Lydon				A. Currier			
A. Farrar				D. Wright			
M. Offiah				D. Myers			
F. Botica		4		J. Davies		3	
S. Edwards				R. Goulding			
K. Skerrett	1			K. Sorensen	1		
M. Dermott				P. Hulme Capt			
A. Platt				H. Howard			
D. Betts				R. Eyres	1		
P. Clarke				E. Faimalo			
D. Bell	1			D. Hulme			
Subs				*Subs*			
S. Panapa	1			Jules O'Neill			
A. Farrell				S. McCurrie			

Referee: R Smith (Castleford)
Half Time: 14-12; Attendance: 77,684

The Homecoming

After the game the players met up with their families in the Banqueting Suite at Wembley before departing on two buses for the reception which was to be held at The Bellhouse Hotel in Beaconsfield.

As the team lost, the reception was quiet at first but after the speeches a disco started but for the majority of the night the dancefloor was pretty empty. Members of the Widnes Supporters Club joined the party as did the Academy players before leaving in the early hours for home.

The next morning the buses were loaded up for the journey home but not before everybody had said their goodbyes to Julian

O'Neill, the young Australian player who had spent a few months playing for the team and had been flown over especially for the Final and was now heading off to Heathrow Airport for his return flight.

As in 1984 the coach pulled into Burtonwood Services on the M62 and the players and wives boarded an open top bus for the remainder of the journey. The bus made its way through the streets of the town before arriving at the Municipal Building where they players were introduced to the large crowd that had turned out to welcome them home.

The Widnes faithful meet to welcome their heroes despite losing to Wigan in the 1993 Challenge Cup Final

A Brief History of Widnes RLFC

The Rugby Football Union was formed in 1872. Whether the Webb-Ellis legend was a factor or not is irrelevant today. What is certain is that the forebears of the present Widnes Club, under the guise of Farnworth and Appleton date from 1873, just one year later.

The history of Widnes Football Club is a story of loyalty and support from the township throughout the early years, when the Club gained no special distinction.

This faith in the future was the beacon which remained undimmed through the uneventful years and has enabled the Club to survive and to emerge from comparative obscurity to its present position amongst the leading clubs in the RL world. Like many other sporting clubs, this early Football and Athletic Club had to endure a somewhat nomadic existence within the town before taking up residence at the Lowerhouse Lane site during the 1895-96 season at what is today the Halton Stadium.

In its early beginnings the rugby was played on unfenced fields firstly where Ross Street now stands, and secondly on the site of the Widnes Technical College. In 1875 the name Farnworth and Appleton was changed to Widnes and a move to an enclosure off Peelhouse Lane was to be home until 1884-85, except for a one season interruption caused by bad drainage.

Below: Arthur ('Chick') Johnson

For that one year a temporary rented home was found at Widnes Cricket Field in Lowerhouse Lane, a site adjacent to the present Halton Stadium but now enveloped by the Kingsway Scheme. Later games in Lowerhouse Lane were played on what is now Leigh Recreation Ground before the Club's Committee was able to purchase the whole field between the Cricket Ground and the north side of Milton Road. This was totally enclosed with a wooden fence and was formally opened with a game against Liversedge on 12th October 1895

Earliest records confirm scarlet and black as the Club's official colours, the strip still favoured by the Widnes RUFC at Heath Road. For reasons not now known the first change was to chocolate and sky blue around the time of the move to Lowerhouse Lane. It was short-lived! Black and white was introduced in 1888-89 using white shirts and black shorts. The traditional black and white hoops with which Widnes became known throughout both the

Left: Widnes RLFC 1908

Northern Union and Rugby League world came in before 1895, the 'breakaway' year, and maintained for over eighty years until Vinty Karalius, coach in the Seventies, sought alternatives, and later sponsorship and replica sales dictated frequently changing designs.

The disputes that had been festering in English rugby for some years came to a head in 1895 and along with twenty one other, typically working class, Northern England clubs Widnes became a founder member of the breakaway Northern Union. The first fixture under the auspices of the Northern Union (NU) was away to Runcorn on 7 September 1895. The game was lost 15-4, the only Widnes points coming from a Rispan drop goal (then worth 4 points). The first NU visitors to Widnes were Leeds on 14th September 1895, the result this time going with Widnes by 11-8.

*Left: Six Widnes players selected for Lancashire circa 1913-14.
Back row (left to right): Sam Aspey, Billy Reid, George Wright (trainer).
Front row: Chick Johnson, Jack O'Garra, George Aspey, Harry Taylor*

Widnes finished that inaugural season in 17th position out of 22 teams winning 14 and drawing 4 of the 42 matches.

Playing improvement was slow. Widnes was not one of the star-studded teams of the times and was generally regarded as a dour side made up of locals from the town's chemical factories, which in turn gave rise to the club's nickname of 'the Chemics'. It was the very parochial nature of the club that over several decades was to fire a local fervour that contrived to weave rugby league football indelibly into the fabric and folklore of the town for all time.

Prior to World War I the names of Billy Reid, Harry Taylor and the two O'Garra brothers, together with the classy 'Chick' Johnson, were all set to become household names. 'Chick' Johnson was the Club's first Great Britain international and his famous dribbled try in the 1914 'Rorke's Drift', deciding, Third Test assured his place in the game's history. Historians still write of this match as simply the most famous match in Test history between Great Britain and Australia. Jack O'Garra also toured in 1914 but was not capped at Test level.

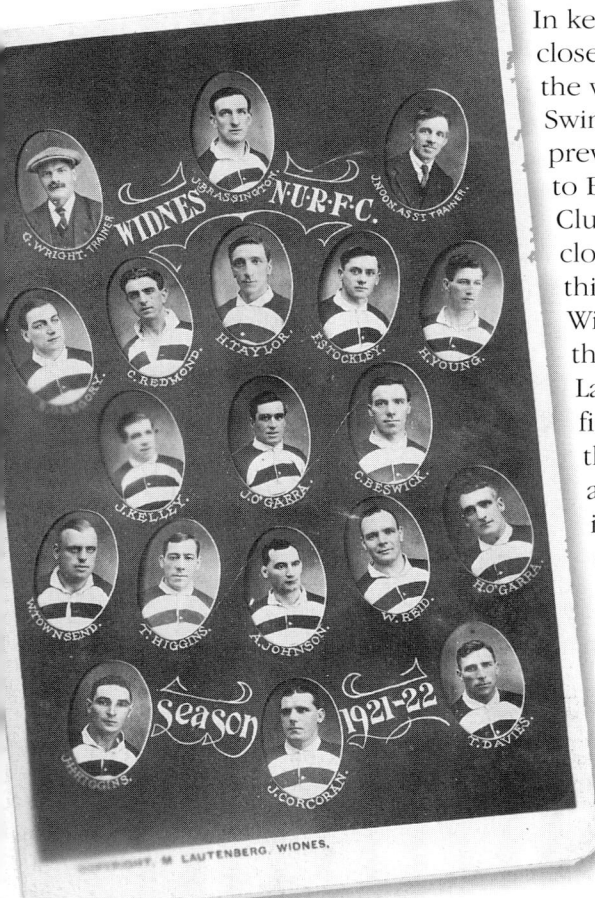

In keeping with most other NU clubs Widnes closed for most of the 1914-1918 period and the war took one notable casualty in Ernie Swinton, a winger who had finished the previous season as second leading tryscorer to Billy Reid. Like many others the Widnes Club emerged from the enforced period of closure in some financial difficulty although this certainly did not translate onto the field. Widnes shocked the NU world by becoming the unlikely winners of the 1919-20 Lancashire League title. This was Widnes' first trophy success and the only occasion they won the now defunct tournament, although Runners Up status was achieved in 1936-37 and 1946-47. The same year (1919-20) the team reached the Semi-Finals of the Lancashire Cup, the third round of the Challenge Cup and the Top Four of the League. By the time the League playoff came around Widnes were without 'Chick' Johnson, again en route to Australia, this time accompanied by Billy Reid, and a Semi-Final exit ensued.

Billy Reid, Tourist, County and International player, before becoming a referee, committeeman and life member of the Club, achieved a rugby immortality in the town, partly perpetuated by the doggerel in the Club's match programme through until his death in the mid-fifties.

> *"Here's to the wearers of black and white,*
> *The men of mighty deeds.*
> *Come drink their health with us tonight,*
> *In the best at Billy Reid's."*

This reference of course was to Reid's Prince of Wales public house, of which ex-player and 1980's Chairman, Ray Owen, was later to be the licensee.

The remainder of the Twenties brought little glory except a double visit of the Australian tourists in 1921-22. Twelve thousand spectators saw Widnes lose the first encounter 28-4, but seemingly so much had the tourists enjoyed the game at Widnes that a repeat was held over the Christmas period of 1921, with the colonials contained this time to 17-8.

As the decade deteriorated from a playing point of view, so problems grew around the continuing tenure at Lowerhouse Lane. The ground, owned by Widnes RLFC, was subjected to a compulsory purchase order by the Town Council with the intention to use the land as part of the developing

Right to left: Paddy Douglas (with Cup), Jimmy Hoey, Harry Millington, Harry Owen Snr, Walter Bradley, Jim 'Dipper' Jones, Frank Bradley, Harry Owen Jnr and Harry Hill get together for Frank Tobin's testimonial game

Above: Widnes RLFC circa 1933

Kingsway Council House Scheme. A five year lease granted in 1926, after much debate with Housing Ministers and Local Government, gave sufficient breathing space for action that was to secure the future.

A Ground Purchase Appeal was launched by the then Secretary, Mr Tom Naughton, to raise £3,250. At the time against the backcloth of industrial depression and mass unemployment hitting the North of England towns more than most, it seemed an unlikely achievement. The consequence of failure was that the club would fold. Encouraged by the Rugby League, who generously agreed to subscribe 10 percent of the total money raised, the Supporters Club and Members undertook a whole series of cash-raising events. One was a soccer match on the ground between a local Merseyside team and the FA Cup Winners, West Bromwich Albion.

A town festival was held in June 1932, with all proceeds going to the Ground Purchase Scheme, and door to door collections took place. No town could have been more committed to keeping its rugby club.

The ground was purchased in August 1932 although, seemingly unreasonably in the light of later ground development constraints, the Council put a condition on the purchase with a buy-back clause at the same price.

This clearly affected attitude towards subsequent major ground work and was not removed until forty years later. Sadly Tom Naughton was to die in a motor accident the same year as his scheme reached fruition the ground was subsequently renamed Naughton Park in memory and in appreciation of the work he had initiated.

In the midst of all the ground activity the team was emerging from the gloom of several disappointing campaigns into what was to be a truly golden era. The 1929-30 season was proving to be only moderate in terms of league results, the financial position was parlous but the Cup run was to elevate the 1930 team to the status of folklore. All Widnesians know the story by heart. Fielding twelve locals plus the giant South African Van Rooyen, obtained on a free transfer seemingly after his career with Hull Kingston Rovers and Wigan was finished, Widnes faced the international packed St Helens, in only the second Final staged at Wembley. St Helens were heavily backed pre-match favourites, they had finished in top-league spot against the modestly placed mid-table Widnes.

For the record Widnes won 10-3 after Saints scored first, and the Widnes team that day was... Bob Fraser; Jack Dennett, Albert Ratcliffe, Peter Topping, Harry Owen; Paddy Douglas (Captain), Jerry Laughton; Fred Kelsall, George Stevens, Nat Silcock, George Van Rooyen, Harry Millington, Jimmy Hoey.

Paddy Douglas became the first Widnes Captain to lift the Cup at Wembley, but the hero of the day, without any doubt, was the 37 year old George Van Rooyen. This success came 57 years after the Club's formation and was the thirtieth year of the Challenge Cup Competition.

It seems Widnes supporters have always been lively at Wembley! 1930 saw the upright scaled and a black and white cap perched on the top of one of the posts.

The Thirties brought two more Wembley visits. The first in 1934 against Hunslet, an unfashionable club from southeast Leeds, who had to play one man short because of injury to centre Morrell for an hour of the match but still won.

Above: The old scoreboard registers one of the most famous victories in the Club's history

Widnes made Wembley history that year with the fielding of 13 players born in the Town - a feat unlikely ever to be repeated by any team. Captain on the day was Nat Silcock, who was to enjoy more success with his 1937 team and victory over Keighley 18-5. The era brought to the fore such great names as Jimmy Hoey, Nat Silcock, Tom McCue, Tom Shannon, Alec Higgins and Harry Millington.

Jimmy Hoey secured his place-in history both local and national by becoming the first player in Rugby League to play and score in every match for his club in one season. This he did in 1932-33 with 40 games, 83 goals and 21 tries. Widnesians at the time though were kept in suspense since the last match was at Barrow and when the score of a loss of 9- 19, Widnes scoring three tries, came through it was assumed Hoey had failed at the last hurdle. Hoey in fact, it was soon learned, had scored all three tries. Jimmy Hoey retired in 1935 but many other players of that time had their careers curtailed or severely interrupted by the onset of World War II.

At the end of May 1940 the Widnes Club shut down for the period of the War as they had done 25 years before. Some players did 'guest' for other teams, notably with Halifax where the triumvirate of Shannon, McCue and Millington played. McCue actually winning a Yorkshire Cup Final medal.

1945-46 brought another post-war boom both to sport in general and to Rugby League and Widnes in particular. The Good Friday home fixture with Warrington attracted a then record ground attendance of 15,466.

The team won the Lancashire Cup with a famous victory over Wigan at Wilderspool and reached the Semi-Final of the Challenge Cup, this time losing to Wigan. It didn't last and as the remnants of the pre-war team made way for newcomers achievements were limited. A Wembley appearance in 1950 against Warrington ending 0-19 was marred by the loss to Widnes of Tourists Naughton and Higgins en route to Australia.

Mention should be made however of the Widnes Captain of the day, Tom Sale, who at 32 had joined Widnes only months earlier that year after deciding to play out his Final years with a Leigh junior club. He thus had the unique distinction of captaining a Wembley side and a Junior club in the same season.

Not only was performance on the field at a low ebb but embryo talent from the town was being lured away. Doug Silcock, Nat's son, and John Broome both chose Wigan, Vin Karalius signed for St Helens and all were to become top class internationals. Broome and Karalius both did eventually end their playing days with the Widnes club. In fact, it was the signing of John Broome as player-coach in 1956 that began the turnaround.

Frank Myler was established as a world class player and younger players from within the town were acquired and such as Ray Owen, Ged Lowe and Billy Thompson were all to play a major part in the Sixties.

Broome left in 1961 but not before a Cup draw at St Helens brought the existing attendance record of 24,205 for the following Thursday afternoon replay. Alex Murphy led the Saints to a 29-10 win.

Joe Egan replaced John Broome as coach and added Rhodesian John Gaydon, Jim Measures and Karalius to his squad. 1961-62 was to be a challenging year; the Rugby League had announced a two divisional scheme for the following season and qualification for the higher grade was vital, Widnes finished in sixth place, their best position since season 1948-49. During that close season Widnes were invited to play in a four-sided tournament in Dublin along with Huddersfield, Workington and Featherstone Rovers. Widnes beat Huddersfield 28-20 to win the Final.

Playing improvements continued over the next two years, albeit there was a long interruption in the big freeze of Winter '62-'63. No games were played from before Christmas up to February and Widnes entered the fray again ahead of most others thanks to the use of an anti-freeze chemical 'GL5' of local manufacture. It was clear at the time that whilst rendering the ground playable it was not conducive to supporting grass growth!

A disappointing Cup exit at home to Hull Kingston Rovers in 1963 seemed to spill over to the following season's league campaign but the shrewd mid-term signings of Alan Briers and particularly big Frank Collier put the club on course for a Cup run that still stands as the longest in Challenge Cup history, involving no less than five replays.

For success-starved Widnesians 1964 Wembley, against Hull Kingston Rovers, was a wonderfully memorable day. Although only a Bob Randall goal separated the two sides at half time defeat was never a consideration and tries by Alan Briers, Frank Myler and Lance Todd winner, Frank Collier, gave Karalius and Widnes the Cup.

As so often happens to successful teams, in any kind of sport, the following year whether anti-climaxal or not was disappointing. A succession of lost matches and numerous players wanting away from the club gave a final League position of only 18th. Of dubious value, the one season 'Bottom 14' Competition operated for that one year only, Widnes going out to the eventual winners, Huddersfield.

In the latter part of the Sixties floodlights were obtained via a public subscription fund at a cost of £9,500 and initiated at the St Helens game on 27th September 1965. The club entered the new BBC2 Television Floodlit Competition - winning it only once, thirteen years later.

The decade ended on a low note. 1966-67 was a dismal playing season. In 1967 the biggest bombshell of all was the sale of Frank Myler to St Helens, Widnes taking £5,500 plus Dave Markey and Ray French. Coach Joe Egan resigned in 1968. In the following season, under new coach Bob Harper the team went through a sequence of ten games without a win and eventually finished fourteenth in the League. In the Challenge Cup that year Widnes played and beat York at Naughton Park in the first ever Sunday match which attracted 8,198 spectators.

Into the Seventies and Don Gullick had come and gone as Bob Harper's successor and in his place came the one man all Widnesians would have chosen, Vinty Karalius. Enthusiasm and expectation were high, the team's performances improved and after some interim disappointment it was Wembley again in 1975.

Twelve months before though had seen the Widnes Club Centenary Year. Finishing fourth in the League and Finalists in the BBC2 Trophy, for the second successive year, only to lose unbelievably at home to a mediocre Bramley side, who had never before or since won a trophy. Because of the power workers strike the 'floodlit' tourney, apart from the first round matches, was played in daylight! Ray Dutton came within one match (the last one) of equalling Jimmy Hoey's scoring feat.

Back to 1975 and despite Karalius' retirement immediately after victory over Warrington, the Wembley victory was to herald a period of success, the manner and extent of which could not have been envisaged.

Under Frank Myler, now returned to the Widnes Club for his first coaching appointment, the team brought its first ever Division 1 Championship to the Town.

Below: Captain Reg Bowden raises the Players No. 6 trophy aloft in 1979

Dubbed the 'Cup Kings' and with Doug Laughton at the helm from 1978 to 1991, except for a mid-eighties spell, the Club won every major honour.

Between 1974-75 and 1990-91 Widnes achieved three Division 1 Championships, seven visits to Wembley with four wins, six Lancashire Cups, two John Player Trophy successes, six Premiership victories, a BBC2 Trophy win, three Charity Shield successes (all against Wigan) and the World Club Championship against Canberra Raiders at Old Trafford in 1989.

Interestingly, in between the two Laughton spells, Karalius returned for another great Wembley triumph in 1984 which will be remembered for the way in which two young Wiganers, Joe Lydon and Andy Gregory, masterminded their home town's downfall.

In the early Nineties, under Frank Myler in his second period, the Club's image was vastly different from its parochial past with a far more cosmopolitan team although local loyalty was undiminished. The Club had made signings that had both boosted playing standards and attracted worldwide media attention.

Below: 'World Champions...' Widnes celebrate on a famous night in the Club's history

Adopted Widnesians included Jonathan Davies, an icon of Welsh Rugby Union, British Lion and Welsh International John Devereux, the giant second row pair, Welshman Paul Moriarty and Tongan Emosi Koloto, Scottish Rugby Union international Alan Tait and the tryscoring sensation from Rosslyn Park, Martin Offiah. Allied to those signings the team could boast as fine an array of local talent as at any time in its past with the likes of Tony Myler, the Hulme brothers, Andy Currier and Richard Eyres...

Above: Captain Kurt Sorensen with the World Club Challenge trophy in 1989

From there it was downhill. World-class players came at a cost that had to be supported and it seemed the Widnes public was satiated by the surfeit of success. The remainder of the nineties decade was characterised more by the political machinations surrounding the formation of Super League, with the Widnes Club's exclusion in 1995, and the financial restructuring of the Club rather than any notable playing successes.

Phil Larder, later to become part of the England RFU coaching establishment, followed Frank Myler as coach and took the Club to Wembley in 1993. The highlight of the cup run was the Semi-Final defeat of Leeds, now managed by Laughton, leading sadly to a disappointing Wembley defeat against a Wigan side that included former Widnes favourites Lydon and Offiah. The 1993 Wembley Final heralded the end of a glorious nineteen-year period.

After Larder came Tony Myler, Doug Laughton for his third spell, Graeme West, Colin Whitfield and David Hulme. None served longer than two years or brought back the success the Club craved, amidst an ever-worsening financial crisis,

The Club was £1.5 million in debt with losses running at £5,000 per week. In attempting to embrace the RFL gospel of 'Framing The Future', ahead of many other clubs, Widnes found that the essential cost cutting on superstar contracts only caused a further downward spiral of playing performances and loss of support.

Rock bottom was reached in 1997 when the Club finished in a relegation position in the first division, below Super League, only to be given a reprieve as the demise of top-flight clubs Oldham and Paris caused the leagues to be reorganised.

Off the field some very serious decisions were made which were to prove crucial in guiding the Club back to the top division.

In May 1993 the Club incorporated moving from a Members Club to a Private Limited Company. A legal challenge to secure a Super League place had failed. The old Naughton Park, badly in need of essential and costly improvements, was sold to Halton Borough Council in 1995, the RFL centenary year, and the site transformed into an 11,000 seater modern stadium, an era gone but fondly remembered.

The deal with the Council was for a sale and leaseback arrangement, initially via a short-lived joint venture company, but eventually to full ownership by HBC and a 35- year lease for the Club.

By 2001, when Neil Kelly was appointed as Coach, the Club had achieved financial stability and his appointment midway through the playing season was part of a determined drive to win promotion to Super League.

Kelly's recruitment of seasoned players, mainly from Yorkshire, brought an end of season 17 from 18 run of victories, which included the Premiership Grand Final and with it a place in Super League VII. Years 2002 and 2003 helped to consolidate the top-flight status with respectable league placings of seventh and ninth.

Below: Martin Crompton celebrates the Vikings' return to the 'big time' in 2001

In 2004, following a run of poor results, Kelly was replaced by New Zealander Frank Endacott who helped guide the team to safety. 2005 has seen the team get off to a poor start but at the time of writing, June 2005, the 2,500 capacity East Stand is near to completion and there has been an upturn in form and with a trip to Toulouse in the Quarter Final of the Challenge Cup at the end of the month there could yet be another chapter for 'Twelve Locals and a South African'.

Compiled by Tom Fleet